Quotes About Michael Toms

". . . one of the best interviewers who has ever worked the American airwaves, radio or TV."

Robert Fuller
Physicist, educator, past president of Oberlin College,
and active citizen diplomat

"Someone with whom I have cruised some important realms of the cosmic ocean and in doing so have developed ever increasing confidence in his intuitive navigation."

R. Buckminster Fuller (1895–1983)
Inventor of the geodesic dome, designer,
philosopher, and creator of the World Game

". . . Bill Moyers and Michael Toms are alike: two of the most creative interviewers it has been my good fortune to work with."

Joseph Campbell (1904–1987)
Mythologist and author of *Hero with a Thousand Faces*, *The Masks of God*, *Myths to Live By*, and *The Mythic Image*

New Dimensions Books

Lynn Andrews
in Conversation with
Michael Toms

Series editor
Hal Zina Bennett, Ph.D.

Published by

Aslan Publishing
Lower Lake, California
USA

Published by
Aslan Publishing
P.O. Box 108
Lower Lake, CA 95457
(707) 995-1861

For a free catalog of all our titles,
or to order more copies of this book,
please call (800) 275-2606.

Library of Congress Cataloging-in-Publication Data

Andrews, Lynn V.
    Lynn Andrews in conversation with Michael Toms.
        p. cm. — (New dimensions books)
    ISBN 0-944031-42-0 : $8.95
    1. Andrews, Lynn V.—Interviews. 2. Shamans—United States—
Interviews. 3. Indians of North America—Religion—Miscellanea.
4. Shamanism. I. Toms, Michael.
II. Title. III. Series.
BP610.A5419A541444 1994
299'.93—dc20   94-11148
[B]   CIP

Cover design by Channing Rudd
Printed in USA

10 9 8 7 6 5 4 3 2 1

Table of Contents

Series Introduction

Through a cooperative arrangement between New Dimensions Radio and Aslan Publishing, we are pleased to present these highly readable introductions to some of the finest and most influential minds of our times. These books grew out of interviews by Michael Toms of the "New Dimensions" radio series, a man who is arguably the most articulate, insightful and well-read radio personality of our times. A non-profit educational organization, New Dimensions Radio has dedicated its efforts to "foster communication about personal and social transformation" through weekly interviews with some of the world's most prominent figures in religion, science, psychology, philosophy, ecology and virtually every other discipline, for over twenty years.

In 1973, Michael and Justine Toms were inspired by a comment made by Charles Tart, a renowned researcher in altered states of consciousness. Tart had remarked that we were "in the midst of the most dramatic shift in human consciousness in the history of the planet—and nobody is paying attention." Convinced that Tart was right, and that the mass media were particularly resistant to what was happening, Michael and Justine stepped boldly forward and launched "New Dimensions," originally through KQED-FM in San Francisco. Michael has served as principal host, with Justine acting as program and series producer.

Today, the "New Dimensions" radio series boasts a broadcast network of nearly two hundred stations throughout the United States and abroad. Together, Michael and Justine have pioneered a new style of "compassionate journalism," which fosters open dialogue and clear communication intended to empower the listener. Their weekly listenership has now reached more than two million worldwide, while the roster of their interviewees includes Nobel Prize physicists, holistic physicians, artists, healers, and notables such as Buckminster Fuller, Joseph Campbell, Black Elk and the Dalai Lama.

Our goal in this series is to offer books that extend the Tomses' ambitious efforts to the printed page, probing the minds of our country's leading thinkers, recording their thoughts and feelings as well as the essence of their own works. In these books, we feel that we have been able to capture more than the intellectual side of the great minds of our generation; in addition, we've been able to catch glimpses of these great minds as people, touched by those events of everyday life that we all know so well. These are books that allow us to share how the most outstanding minds incorporate their ideas into their own daily life processes.

By virtue of the more informal interviews which are the basis of these books, we catch brief glimpses into the doubts, fears and private aspirations that interviewees have expressed. These candid insights are rarely found in more formal books or lectures. They are important because they help us humanize works that we might otherwise think are beyond our own capacities. In this way, the *great works* of our time become much more accessible, much more "user friendly" and applicable in our own lives.

At the time the publisher came to me with the idea for this series, I had been an avid listener of New Dimensions radio programming since its inception. I had even enjoyed the honor of being interviewed by the Tomses over the years, talking about books I had either authored or co-authored. But most important of all, the interviews I heard on that series were often my introduction to the real giants at the cutting edge of science, psychology, the social sciences, spirituality, the arts and self-development.

From the beginning, we have all been excited by the opportunity to present in this highly readable form ideas that are helping to make this a better world. It is our hope that whether you are reading these ideas for the first time, or have picked up this book to refresh your memory of a lecture, book or workshop that previously introduced you to these authors, lecturers and teachers, that you will be moved as profoundly as we have been by their efforts.

Throughout our publishing program, we continue to dedicate ourselves to bringing you the works of men and women who are amongst the most creative, thought-provoking, and controversial on this planet. We hope you will look for other books in this series, since together they present the ideas that are truly changing the world for the better.

—Hal Zina Bennett, Ph.D.

Introduction

Lynn Andrews began her path of self-discovery and enlightenment nearly twenty years ago. Since the publication of her first book, *Medicine Woman,* in 1981 she has chronicled her incredible journeys into the self in a number of books, three of which have been *New York Times* bestsellers.

Over the years, Lynn has gained a worldwide following and is considered a preeminent teacher in the field of personal development. She is recognized as a shaman, which she defines as a wounded healer who has lived through a life-challenging situation and has come out of the experience with special capabilities.

Describing survivors of dysfunctional families and abuse as "the shaman initiates of the twentieth century," her life and work are devoted to healing the planet by first healing the individual. Although her books have centered on the theme of women and feminine consciousness, her message speaks to both sexes and all ages. Her journeys over the past two decades have taken her around the world, where she has studied with women of power from various shamanic traditions.

While many of her teachers are Native American, Lynn insists that it is neither her purpose nor intent to teach traditional tribal ways. Rather, she sees her work as a weaving together of ancient and contemporary thought, the purpose being to reawaken us to the mysteries of life and to help us grasp a deeper appreciation for our own individual power.

Lynn's books include: *Flight of the Seventh Moon; Jaguar Woman; Star Woman; Crystal Woman; Windhorse Woman; Teachings Around the Sacred Wheel; The Woman of Wyrd; The Mask of Power; The Power Deck; Shakkai—Woman of the Sacred Garden,* and *Woman at the Edge of Two Worlds: The Spiritual Journey of Menopause.*

▲

Section One

▼

Medicine Woman

MICHAEL: *Deep within our hearts each of us is longing for something more. We may ask, is this all there is? Then we blindly continue our headlong pace, looking neither to the right nor to the left. But once in a while we break away from the well-traveled path and find a different way to live our lives, one that is new yet remarkably old as well. We find the spiritual journey beckoning to the deepest part of us. Though the inner voice that calls us is sometimes soft, sometimes distant, the call is always powerful.*

Lynn Andrews is a person who answered just such a call and whose life was transformed in the process. The story of how that occurred has fascinated her readers for many years. But because of the note it strikes in all our hearts we never tire of hearing it again. Could you tell us your story one more time, Lynn? Where did it start? When did you first realize that there had to be something more in your life? When did you begin to feel that perhaps the life you were living wasn't all there was for you?

LYNN: I think I have always had a sense that something was missing in my life, that I wanted to always grow. But in some ways, I have to say that I've always been one of those lucky people who has always been able to follow my dreams. I was living in Los Angeles, where I was dealing in Native American art and was a collector myself. I was most interested in magical objects and fetishes of all kinds. I had been particularly attracted to a fertility sash that I had heard was somewhere in Guatemala. I decided to go down there and try to find it.

I had made arrangements to meet a particular trader in Guatemala City. However, when I arrived there I was told he had gone to Tikal. So one early morning I flew into Tikal, far into the jungles.

Tikal is a fantastic Mayan ruin, covering fifty square miles. I got out of the plane and went in search of the trader. Once again, I was told that he had been there but had already flown back to Guatemala City. Since my plane had already taken off, leaving me stranded, I had little choice but to make the most of it. I decided to spend the day exploring the ruins.

There was absolutely no one there. It was magnificent. I was so fascinated with everything I saw that I became totally disoriented among the ruins. I wandered around for what seemed like hours, then bumped into an Indian man who was just standing there. He seemed to have appeared out of nowhere. I turned to him immediately, hopeful that he might speak English. I asked him how to get back to the airport.

Much to my relief, he did speak some English and ended up taking a great deal of time talking with me. He knelt down, drew a circle in the dirt, and explained how to get back to the airport, which was really quite complicated. When he was finished, I felt I should give him something for being so kind to me. All I had in my purse was a twenty dollar bill, so I handed him that.

He took it, looked at me strangely, then tore the bill in half. Handing half the torn bill back to me he said, "This money binds us. Put it in your bundle. You belong in the North. Within the next forty-four days I will send you a male and female helper."

I thought this very strange. I didn't know why he was going to send me a male and female helper. Nor did I know what he meant by a bundle. Nevertheless, I put my half of the bill behind a credit card in my wallet. I thought, gee, this guy must be crazy!

"Don't ever come back here to this spot," he told me. At that, he turned and disappeared into the jungle.

With the aid of the man's directions I easily found my way back to the airport. Although it had been a curious encounter, I really didn't think any more about the man. When I finally got back to Guatemala City, I made the necessary contacts, got hold of the trader I'd been trying to track down and attained the fertility sash I'd come for. After that, I returned to Los Angeles and went about my business.

About two weeks after returning, I happened to be at an exhibition of Stieglitz black and white photographs at a local gallery, viewing a collection of work that I found very interesting. I was with a friend who didn't share my enthusiasm for Stieglitz' work at all. In fact, he let me know in no uncertain terms that he found the show terribly boring. He wanted to leave and so kept dragging me toward the door.

Upon his insistence, I had little choice but to leave sooner than I otherwise would have. But as we were leaving I noticed a particular photograph out of the corner of my eye. I stopped to get a closer look. It was a sepia print of a beautiful Native American basket. For some reason I was very drawn to it. I was so fascinated that I stood there for several minutes. I thought how unlike Stiegletz this photo was. I went up to it and touched it with my hands and my hands dissolved into the photograph and I jumped back. While it was a picture of a Native American basket, it was different from any basket I had ever seen. It looked sort of coiled and it had a dolphin design and one of lightning on it. Under the photo I saw a little sign. It said, "Marriage Basket," circa eighteen hundred-and-something. The photographer was one I'd never heard of before—a person by the name of McKinnley.

I stood there admiring the photo for some time and decided I wanted to buy it. But when I told my friend, he was anxious to go, and said, "Come back and buy it on your own time. Let's get out of here."

So we left.

That night began a series of incredible dreams. I dreamed of the basket in the photograph. It was being handed to me by this ancient Native American woman. I kept waking up, feeling that it was urgent that I go back to the gallery and buy the photograph. Needless to say, I got very little sleep that night. The next morning I called the gallery, told them who I was and said I wanted to come down immediately and purchase the photograph of the basket by McKinnley that I had seen hanging on their wall the day before. I asked them to please hold it for me. There was a bit of confusion on the other end of the phone line, and a minute later the woman I'd been talking to said, "We don't have a photograph like the one you're describing. We have no record of it whatsoever. Are you sure you saw it here?"

"I'm absolutely positive," I said. "I was there with a friend of mine yesterday."

"I'm sorry," the woman said. "I'm sure we have never had such a photograph."

I hung up the phone in exasperation. There was not a bit of doubt in my mind that I had the right gallery and that I had seen the photograph there. I immediately got dressed and rushed down to the gallery, racing inside and going directly to the wall where I'd seen the photo. Just as they'd told me on the phone, they had no such photograph. There was no sign of it whatsoever! I asked to go through their files, meticulously examining them, looking under the name of the artist, the description of the photo, and every other way I could imagine. But there clearly was no record of such a photo. So I went home. I got to thinking about the photo and the dream and called the friend who'd been with me in the gallery the day before, who happened to be a psychiatrist. I asked him, "Do you remember that photograph of the Indian basket I saw yesterday?"

"No," he said, "I don't." He kind of laughed at me and jokingly said, "Maybe you'd better make an appointment to come in and see me."

But I told him I was fairly certain I wasn't crazy.

Every night for another week or so, I dreamed of the basket I'd seen in the photo. I just couldn't get it out of my mind.

I had to have it, or at least find out more about it. I called collectors and dealers all over the country trying to find someone who might know about it. I found many people who'd heard of a marriage basket but nobody seemed to know exactly what it was. I wasn't getting anywhere in my search.

Then one night at a party in Los Angeles, absolutely the most unlikely place in the world, I ran into a Native American medicine man. It turned out to be Grey Wolf, who was the author of a well-known book on legends. He was wonderful. We talked and there was a real connection made between us. During the course of the evening I asked him if he had ever heard of a marriage basket.

"Yes," he said, "I do know about a marriage basket, I know of just one in existence. It is located in Canada. Why do you ask?"

I told him my story about the photograph and my dreams about this old woman handing me the basket and how I had become totally obsessed with finding this basket. "I really need to find out what it's all about," I told him.

"It is a very dangerous object and very sacred," he said, trying to dissuade me.

I really pressed him and finally he said, "You can go to Ruby Plenty Chiefs in Manitoba, Canada. If she is willing, and if she finds you worthy, she will send you to the keeper of the basket, who is Agnes Whistling Elk."

He gave me Agnes Whistling Elk's general location and I went to Canada to find Ruby Plenty Chiefs. I went to her in a sacred way, with an offering of a blanket and some tobacco. When I found Ruby, she put me through an incredible ordeal until she finally felt I was worthy. She told me I had to hike nine miles due east to Agnes's cabin, which I did.

When I found Agnes I was stunned. She was the woman I'd seen in my dreams who had held the basket out to me night after night! I told her I'd been dreaming of her and she kind of giggled. When I told her I wanted to buy the marriage basket she laughed at me. She said that the marriage basket could not be bought or sold. There was only one way to get it. It had to be earned.

Just as Grey Wolf before her had done, Agnes told me the basket was a sacred object, woven by the dreams of all women. She said it was woven by the dreamers. She proceeded to tell me that she had been coming to me in my dreams. When I asked her why, she told me that I was a Rainbow Warrioress in this lifetime. When I asked her what this meant, she said it meant that I was to be a bridge between the primal world and social consciousness. As such, I had much to learn. She told me that if I chose to do this I could go into a position of learning with her. She told me to go back to Los Angeles and think about this because, as she said, "If you work with me your life will be changed forever." I followed her advice and returned to the West Coast.

When I got back home, I thought a lot about what had happened. I had no way to make sense of it. There was no doubt in my mind that I had seen that first photograph of the marriage basket on the wall of the gallery, though nobody else could confirm that it had really been there. In addition, I knew for certain that Agnes was the woman I had met in my dreams. While I had no way to explain what had happened, I realized that something special was taking place and she was giving me the opportunity to experience a deeper truth than I'd ever known.

The more I thought about it, the more I realized there really was no decision to be made. I knew that I had to do this. How I knew this, I can't say, because if somebody had asked me at that time, define yourself, who are you as a woman, I would have been stuck for an answer. I really didn't know who I was and so the decision to work with Agnes had to be made out of complete innocence.

For as long as I can remember, I have always been on a search for more. I knew there was more to my life, as you said in the beginning, Michael. And I had never been satisfied by being defined by other people's perceptions or expectations.

I went back to Agnes and began my life of apprentice-ship. When I arrived she stripped me of everything I thought I knew, everything that was familiar. You know, she put me in a situation that was very tough at the time. She was very rough on me at first and so was Ruby. Later Agnes explained that she put me in a hypersensitive situation so that the things she was going to teach me would forever be imprint-ed indelibly in my heart and mind.

One day Agnes called me in and told me she had some-thing important to tell me. She said I was ready to earn the marriage basket. She told me that the basket is a symbol but it is also a real basket.

I must tell you that all her teachings are very experiential. She would guide me into situations in such a way that I would have to experience them directly. She never told me ahead of time what the lesson would involve or what I would learn from it. Rather, I had to live through each situation and perform and learn my lessons. There was no way out except to just go into it and work my way through whatever came up.

Much of the time I felt as if I was caught in an endless labyrinth in which there seemed to be no way out. Agnes said the marriage basket symbolized the relationship between the warrior and warrioress within me. As a woman, she said, I have that most perfect warrior within me which I can project out onto the world. But if I am not mated with that warrior within me, then my relationships, marriages, any of my friendships are going to be incomplete because I myself am not reflected as a complete person. So all of this was involved with earning that marriage basket and it was a very special situation.

I soon discovered that I was pitted against Red Dog. He was a sorcerer who had stolen the marriage basket from Agnes Whistling Elk. He was a totally male person, with none of the feminine shield whatsoever. One of Agnes's teachings was that if you are totally male or totally female you are very dangerous. There are those people who say that Grey Wolf is very dangerous. Actually he is not, because he is totally balanced in his male and female shields. But Red Dog had chosen to be totally male, to work only with that power. He could not deal with the feminine in himself. Nor could he deal with the feminine shield in Agnes Whistling Elk, who had been his teacher at one point.

When you say dangerous, do you mean he could really do physical harm to you?

That's right, he could. He is a very dangerous sorcerer. And for my teaching, Agnes Whistling Elk put herself into the role of the totally female sorceress or medicine woman. So I had to weave my way through the paradox of those two people. I had to survive the challenges they presented to me and balance my energies between them. And that was my journey with Agnes for the first seven years—learning how to balance my energies through the many obstacles I encountered trying to gain back the marriage basket.

One day, we got on some horses and went out into the forest, where we found a meadow. Agnes asked me to dismount and said we were going to have a picnic, which was really unexpected because she had been very hard on me for days and days and days. As we sat there in the grass she asked me, "Lynn, what do you believe in?"

And I said, "Well, I guess I believe in being honest."

Agnes took a rock and placed it in front of me. And then she said, "Okay, what else do you believe in?"

I replied, "I believe in the Great Spirit."

Agnes put another rock in front of me. Then she went through everything I believed in and by the time I was through I had a pile of rocks about three feet high. She proceeded to tell me that these rocks represented my belief structures and that they were fences around my consciousness. She explained that I could not go beyond those fences because we limit ourselves so terribly by what we think we believe in—thinking that we are being good, that we are being true to our spirit, and so on. She said, what we believe limits our input from the universe.

She said, now look at this, this is what you have inside of you. As I looked at the pile of rocks, all I could see was this black mass, the structure inside me that I had to break through. We then got on our horses and rode through the rocks, scattering them in all directions. It was a wonderful experience because I felt a true release, letting go of things that had been limiting my perceptions.

What about power objects and animal helpers? In your books you speak of a wolf. What was that about?

I made a wolf fetish. One day Agnes gave me my medicine. She explained that every person has a spirit animal, a counterpart which...

You're saying every person...meaning all of us?

Yes, all of us. We're not aware of this because a lot of us don't have shaman teachers in our lives. But it's not really unlike astrology, in the sense that you are an Aries and that's represented by the ram and so forth. But a shaman teacher will look at you and see your innermost nature, and will perhaps see that you are a wolf, a bear, a mountain lion, or some other animal. And all are positive; it's just that the animal helps you understand yourself. The psychiatrist will tell you that you had an unhappy experience with your parents and that you are failing in this and that and the other and in your ability to love because of your past conditioning. Instead of going into that, a shaman will see your medicine and give you that power animal and then you begin to work with something tangible. When working with the sacred wheels, we find there are animals in all four directions on the wheel, and each one represents a different power, a different way of viewing the world.

When Agnes gave me my medicine, it was a black wolf, which means that I am an introspective wolf. A wolf is a pathfinder. A path chief will often have wolf medicine because a wolf will guide you through the trails of the universe. The wolf path is the Milky Way in the stars. Does this help to answer your question?

You're answering it. What you're saying is that the spirit animals are like our co-workers on our path.

Yes. They are your helpers and if you can learn to contact the wolf or bear or whatever your medicine is, it helps you on your way. You begin to see who you are. I think one of the most important things of all is to see who you are as a person. There are many ways to do that. The sacred wheel is a wonderful way of teaching that. Agnes really gave me tremendous strength to allow me to find myself as a woman, to help me realize my true center. One of the most powerful gifts she used was giving me my power animal.

Lynn, what were some of the practical matters, the logistics associated with going to Canada and studying with a shaman woman? I mean did you set up a tent? Did you—how did that actually manifest?

It was cold! Much of the time I stayed in Agnes's cabin and worked one-on-one every day, day and night. It was very intense. It was very good because I was lifted out of my usual environment so totally that the possibility of transformation was there. You know, I look at the astronauts who are shot off into the sky to wander around the universe in a tin can. Three or four days later, they come back enlightened or they have suddenly developed powers of ESP. At the very least, they come back with new visions in their life. I think the reason for that is that they have been ripped out of their ritualistic lives, lives that we all have. We travel around by rote. You know, you live in your house for two weeks and you don't see it anymore. The vacuum cleaner can be sitting in the living room and you just walk around it, hardly knowing it's there. And if you have that chance to lift yourself out of your everyday situation long enough so that you can change your mood, it inspires a kind of awe and mystery that you come back with: a complete, new vision of who you are and a new understanding of the value of your life. And I don't think it necessarily means that you have to go to the reservation or that you need to study with a guru or medicine person. But you can read. Reading is a fantastic way to lift yourself into another world, long enough, I think, to bring about change.

Somewhere, you speak of the awe and the mystery. That is certainly present in what you describe. Why are the awe and mystery important?

Awe and mystery are important because they change the mood. We're locked into a mood that's almost irreversible, one that blocks us from seeing what our lives are about. And if you can change that mood in some way, even for a few hours, you come back with the possibility of a new light in your life.

I was curious. Are the group of people that surrounded you before you worked with Agnes the same ones who are in your life now? Or did your experiences change you in such a way that the people in your life also changed?

There are many new people in my life, of course. But I also have all my old friends—most of them, anyway. I think what happens when you begin to actualize yourself, begin to realize your full potential as a human being, is that you begin to see more potential in others. They are a mirror for you and you are a mirror for them. You see in other people what you are yourself. When we come to understand this, all the people in our lives become more important to us. We have a much deeper relationship than we ever had because we have begun to see the many ways we mirror each other.

It amazes me that you're still living in Los Angeles after this experience!

Everybody tells me that, but you know, I have a wonderful house up in the canyons. I have coyotes that come down and literally press their noses against the bedroom window at two in the morning when I'm sitting there writing. I mean they leave little marks on the windows. And I have owls and I have five deer that live in my backyard. I really see more wildlife, believe it or not, in Los Angeles, than I do anywhere else, including in Canada. Los Angeles is my home. I have a daughter there, and I have lived there a long time. I'm not an Indian. I could never live on the reservation all the time. I don't think it would be appropriate or good for me to do that. I think what my purpose in life is, it seems as it's unfolding, is to write about my experiences. That has been such a wonderful gift. I want to teach and help others as I have been helped and taught. I wish that I could give to everybody. The experience with Agnes Whistling Elk and the Sisterhood of the Shields has been truly magical and I learned a lot of powerful things, particularly for women, I think. Certainly not exclusively for women, but women do need to realize that their place is in the home and the whole world is their home, and they need to bring that feminine energy into the world, particularly now. I think that we're so worried about nuclear holocaust and earthquakes and disease, we don't know if we're going to be around for another week, another year or for an eternity. Mostly, we're all beginning to wonder how we got into this position. The Sisterhood of the Shields is concerned with that balance in the universe and harmony! Agnes talks a lot about how women need to learn that they can be as powerful as men and still retain their femininity.

As we look at the different institutions and look at the boards of directors of the major companies, it's amazing how few women we find in positions of power in our society.

Yes. And the world is in desperate need of that feminine power. We need women to realize that they can give men power. Men have to realize that they can get so much power from women. It's all interrelated. Woman can destroy man but in destroying him she destroys herself.

There is a quote from Agnes Whistling Elk in your book Medicine Woman: *"There are no medicine men without medicine women. The medicine man is given power by a woman and it has always been that way. Medicine man stands in the place of the dog.*

He is merely an instrument of woman. It doesn't look that way any-more, but it is true."

Yes. At the present time we don't see this because the world is so much out of balance. The place of the dog is the position of high guardianship.

When you speak of balance, of the male and female energies on the planet, it brings up many questions. Maybe you can talk further about the balancing of energies.

Yes. One time Agnes was telling me that the balancing of energies is important. I said, what do you really mean by that? And she said that in each person you have male and female energy. If you take your hands and form a pyramid, with the right hand, you have the male reconstructive energy and in the left hand you have the female creative energy. And both of these energies can be positive or they can be negative. The reconstructive energies are positive in terms of tearing down old habits and tearing down an old building before you build anew. And while the creative energy is very positive, it also can be negative if you have creativity without purpose. Creativity without purpose truly goes nowhere. You need to take these energies and blend them so that you are a total person, so that you can realize your full potential. I think a lot of women do creative things but they do them to stay busy. They don't do them with a real awareness and purpose and that's really important. Agnes told me one time that one of the most important things for a man or a woman to do, to realize or actualize themselves, in psychological terms, is to make an act of power in the world. By making an act of power, she meant doing something long enough, centering and focusing your energy long enough so that regardless of what the project is it becomes a mirror for who you really are. From it you can begin to understand who you are.

So you're saying that whether the project is successful or not may be less important than the fact that it's mirroring back your truth to you, your truth about who you are.

That's really what the importance is. Life is a lesson. We're here to learn something. I really believe that. (Laughs.) That's one of my rocks, as Agnes said. It is important to make that act of beauty or act of power, no matter what it might be. It's important to stretch your boundaries.

This is very exciting to me. You're saying that it's the process that's important. It's the sticking with it long enough that it can become our mirror to be able to discover who we are. For many of us, I think, as soon as it looks like it's going to get a little shaky, a little rough, we just start closing down and walk away. We quit before we have created our mirror.

That's right. That's what I came away with in my apprenticeship with Agnes, for instance. For me I came away from Agnes Whistling Elk an author. I made an act of power, an act of beauty, in the sense that I wrote a book and I'm writing others as sequels. You don't necessarily have to write a book. It could be painting a painting. It could be taking care of your children in a real, aware, conscious way. It could be building a business or becoming a plumber or a photographer.

You also talked in your book about complication and opposition. You said, in this society we're full of competition. We use a lot of energy competing with one another. And what have you learned about competition through your work with Agnes?

Well, first of all I learned that as a woman I was not in competition with anyone, certainly not with men, that I had defined myself as a woman, for myself. In the shaman world they have this wonderful concept of the worthy opponent. Say I were to take Anais Nin, whom I've loved a lot, as my worthy opponent. She was a beautiful writer. Say I wanted to take her on as an opponent, that I had to live up to her power as a woman and as a writer. Say I wanted to be as powerful as she could be. My efforts to do this, to accomplish this difficult task, cause me to reach into myself, to get hold of my power. In other words, the worthy opponent helps you grow. We think of such a competitor with love. Rather than thinking in terms of beating that person, of winning over them, as we tend to do in this society, we have tremendous gratitude and love for them because they guide us to our power.

So you're saying that there is no scarcity of power or success in life. If someone is living successfully, and you relate to them as a worthy opponent, it doesn't mean we take a piece of them and bring them down, or make them less so we can be more.

Oh no! The more they are, the more you are. The more powerful they are the more powerful you are. It's wonderful. You know, by the old way, when a warrior came to a neighboring camp, say the camp of an enemy, he was always put up in the best tepee. He was given the best food and the best people came to visit him. The next day he would choose a worthy opponent and they would use a coup stick. They wouldn't fight to the death. They would fight to humiliate one another, perhaps. Maybe the victor would cut a lock from the hair of his opponent and humiliate him. But this was also a position of great honor. It was never done in the sense that we think of enemies today.

If we could take that out from the micro to the macro level and relate it to nations, you see other nations as the enemy. You fail to see them as the worthy opponent. You fail to see how your worthy opponent can serve you.

Yes, to see it only in the sense of destroying the other is a projection of ego, in a sense. The ego believes it can only be safe by destroying whatever seems to stand in its way.

Could you talk about it from that level for a moment? What does it mean when one nation defines another as an enemy?

The belief is that we must overpower them. We project ego into the world to the point where we are destroying our-selves. If you don't deal in terms of ego, but deal in terms of growth and growth potential, of becoming a magnificent human being, evolving into something beyond mere human strength, you could never think in terms of killing. I think that's the reason Agnes is so interested in having me write books and having other women come out into the world because we need that feminine, intuitional, creative side of the nature. If you think of the world as a body, the body of the world has the male and female energies in it and we have developed the male aggressive side almost totally, to the exclusion of the other. We have not allowed the power of the female to come through. I think Robert Graves said some-thing wonderful. He said that if you suppress the female power in the world you breed a kind of intellectual homo-sexuality, and I think that's what has happened.

In reading your books I was really struck by how you really did bring out the feminine. You really did speak to the female. But like most of us sitting there working in our daily jobs, commuting to work, or working in our homes in some sort of artistic project, completely caught up in a world which is predominantly male, the male values and projections, let's face it, we read something like this and it just sounds like a fairy tale, not something we mere mortals could have in our lives.

You know, I think kind of to the contrary. I think we'll lead incredibly magical lives if we can just open our eyes to see the extraordinary mystery that we are. If we can just realize that we all have an Agnes Whistling Elk, we all have a Ruby Plenty Chiefs or a sorcerer, maybe, that is our boss that we don't get along with. But whoever they are, they are really mirrors, they're teachers. If we could just see that, if only for a moment!

If that's true, we can all set it up just as Lynn set it up. She had a real shaman woman, and she went up to Canada and went to a reservation. But we don't need to be imitative. I tend to think that I can only do it if I follow this recipe to the letter, and I have these ingredients. What you are saying is that each one of us can make up our own recipes. My shaman woman might be the woman next door, or even a woman who comes to me in my dreams. And instead of going to the reservation, maybe it is going to the seashore or to the mountains with a friend.

Oh, yes, there are as many recipes as there are people in this world. I think one of the reasons I wrote my first book the way that I did was so that people could experience what I've experienced, through the reading. I don't think that people have to do anything but just truly become aware in their lives. You don't need to go to an Indian reservation. That is just my path. I am wonderfully happy that I have been blessed in this way, but I don't think that what I do is for everybody. There are many ways in the world and many paths. But remember that we are of this time and of this soil. I asked Agnes one time, what are tools for enlightenment for woman? She replied that women and men need to put a circle of power at their own feet. I said what do you really mean by that? She said, you need to be centered. You need to actualize yourself through an act of power, which we talked about a little while ago. She said, never take power from someone else's circle. Be responsible for your own energy, in other words. And we all have tools. We can all pray. We can all meditate. You don't necessarily have to use shaman ways. I use my shaman things because those are the things I was taught to use and I think it is a most powerful path of heart. But other people maybe who are not interested in the shaman path, maybe they are interested in Buddha—they can meditate. But use the things that you have. So often people have them and they just simply let them lie there unused, sometimes for a lifetime.

How could you take power from someone else's circle as you said?

Well, being overly reliant on someone else, for example. Depending on their perceptions of you, for instance. In other words, I'm a good person if they say I am; I am a bad person if they say that this is so. That's what it feels like when you're on the inside, when you've put yourself into the position of having your power taken away in exchange for relying on other people to determine who you are. Being dependent in some way for support. I think we need to stand on our own two feet.

One of the aspects of shamanic culture that is so important is the sacred wheel. Could you talk about that, what this symbol is for shamanic teaching, and how it might apply to our own lives?

Yes. The sacred wheel is a symbol of the unity of the universe. It also is a wonderful process for understanding, psychologically, where you are in your Earth walk. Let's take the example of a person who is very unhappy in their job. That person might go to Agnes and sit at the sacred wheel to try to find a path out of their present situation. At this sacred wheel there are four directions. There is the north, which is spirit. There is the south, which is physical, in this particular wheel, although there are many sacred wheels. In the west is woman and emotions. In the east is the rational, logical, where most men live. The self stands at the center, in this case. So the person standing at the center is this person who is very unhappy in their job. Essentially they are living in the west, completely caught up in the emotion that they are unhappy. Agnes might then take them to the south, to the physical, and she would ask, "How are you feeling physically?" The person might say, "Well, I think I have an ulcer."

For this particular person, we now have a picture of where they stand in relation to the west and the south. In our society we essentially bounce back and forth between the rational, the emotional and the physical, or the east, the west and the south. The men live in the east pretty much, in their minds. The women live in their emotions. Occasionally they get together in the south for a physical encounter and they kind of go through their life in that fashion. The problem is that they don't go in a full circle. Agnes and Ruby try to teach others to live in a circular fashion, so that they can use all of what they are as a person. What's missing is the experience of spirit in the north.

Let's go back now to this person who is being miserable in their job and having an ulcer. Agnes would take them around the circle and to the north. She would say, "Now, how can we solve this problem?" Finally you begin to realize, with wisdom, that the job is causing the problem. The boss is causing discomfort and stress in this person's life. At this point, Agnes might have this person go to the east, where we use the rational approach to identify the various issues involved and alter the situation. You simply have to quit the job and find a new boss and a new situation, instead of bouncing back and forth between the physical and the emotional, being upset and trying to please a boss who can't be pleased. The shaman woman takes you around the circle so that you can more clearly see the problem and solve it. Through the sacred wheel, the person is able to lift him- or herself out of that problem, the ulcer goes away and they're no longer miserable.

How do we move around the wheel? How do we get into the north, for instance?

The north represents spirit. You cannot get to spirit without first going to the physical and moving around the wheel. The physical is in the south and you then move to the north. But you have to be in touch with your body. You have to be in touch with your total physical being first.

It's not just a mental process.

No. We can learn much from reading, for example, which is a mental process. It's a good way, but it is only a small piece.

We all collect so much knowledge in our heads, both men and women. But how do we become aware on a deeper level? How do we manifest the deeper knowledge you're talking about? All this collection of knowledge that we have in our heads obviously isn't enough. In fact, it seems to actually get in our way a lot of the time. How do we manifest the deeper wisdom? What's the key? Do you have any suggestions?

One of the very best ways is making that act of power in the world that we spoke of. It takes you out of yourself enough, into focused energy, into a centered, actual process, so that you can begin to see who you are. And when you begin to see who you are, you begin your journey to the north, to wisdom.

For instance, let's say you get into a financial jam and can't pay your bills. One day, three people arrive at your house and start dragging out your refrigerator, on which you are six payments behind. In the process, they're tearing the place up, breaking tiles, gouging the woodwork, making a huge mess. In addition, you've got sixteen people coming for dinner that night, and all the food is already prepared and in the refrigerator. Well, you panic. You absolutely freak out. What are you going to do with all these people and no refrigerator!

If you have worked on your center, and you have some of the discipline that comes out of experiencing yourself in the act of power, you recognize a number of things. First, you recognize that you are presently centered in the west, the place of emotion. You also know that this problem cannot be solved by having your efforts focused only on that place. You know that you must turn your center to the east, to the rational, and to the south, the physical.

As you see where your attention is centered, you begin to see that you do not have to limit yourself to this panic. You move your center to the east, toward the rational, to draw upon the knowledge you have in your brain for solving this problem. Then you are able to shift to the south, to focus on the physical, your own body, or physical center, as well as the problem of how to pull off the dinner party, with or without the refrigerator. From your experience with an act of power, you are able to know how you panic, how you react under stress, and you'll know what to do to move out of that center toward integrating all four directions on the sacred wheel, including spirit. You begin realizing your full potential.

On one level, then, we can relate to everything that's happening as a lesson, part of the process of moving toward wisdom, of integrating the different centers on the wheel. From that perspective, it's not the outcome that is important, whether the refrigerator is gone and the dinner party is busted up, so much as how you work with the wheel and your own power at this time.

That's right.

It's seeing how you were feeling and how you responded to that situation that's the most important thing.

Yes. It's how you react as a human being, to have the dignity to work on yourself to the point where you realize your full potential.

Well, most of us get totally into the problem and fail to see it as an opportunity.

Yes. Because we get completely lost in the west, in the emotion. We completely forget what we are doing here on our Earth walk. We panic and we get angry. And the result is that we're not very effective in the world at that point.

I think people fear the impression they are giving to others, like, in that example you just gave, we're really afraid of what the guests will think of us if they arrive and there is no food. I can see in my mind's eye what a wonderful thing that could be; all those people show up and you say, "Yes, isn't this great. We're going to camp out on the living room floor." And it might be the best party you've ever given. But that fear of what other people think of us, maybe you can talk about that for a moment. So many times we get paralyzed in these situations.

We do get paralyzed. There's no question about it. Agnes often worked with me on that. I was filled with fear when I went to work with her and I've not totally overcome that. She showed me my fear in every aspect. When she gave me my wolf medicine, she asked me to go out and make the wolf fetish. She said, now you feel that wolfness within you, you feel the nature of that animal, you see what that means to you: now I want you to make a fetish that is a symbol of all that you are.

I went out and I got wood and collected pieces of string and pieces of horsehair and feathers. I carved this creature, trying to make it as close to what I was feeling inside as I could. I wrapped it and thought it was wonderful and beautiful. Then I brought it to her, proffered it like a child looking for its mother's approval. She got very stern with me. She looked at it and said, "Now, can you read this? Can you see the person who made that?"

She saw how it was wrapped and she told me it was made by a person who lived a lot in the right brain, a perfectionist. She told me, "You certainly believe in beauty and you have a great appreciation of it." She went on and on about how she felt I perceived her as a person through this wolf doll and how it was made. I think that is a really good thing for people to do. It doesn't necessarily have to be a fetish. It can be just a symbol in the physical world of who you think you are spiritually. Just make something that is representative of you. Something like a kachina. It's a very positive and good thing to do, anybody can do that. It doesn't make any difference what you believe in. But once you make that and you set it out in front of you and read it, you begin to understand that it reflects something about you.

You said something about a kachina, that being like a little doll?

Yes, it becomes a physical counterpart of the spiritual part of you. It is a very good thing to do because you can see it physically. Let it stay there for several days and just look at it and study it and you can begin to see your reality. You can see the phoniness in you and you can see your imperfections and the things you need to work on. And the strengths, too, of course. A lot of us don't know what we have to do to work on ourselves. We know that something is missing but we don't know what that is, we don't know how to define it. Certainly the shaman path helps us define it.

How has your life changed since you started studying with Agnes? Can you identify these changes, in very practical, down-to-earth ways?

I think my values have changed tremendously. When I left Los Angeles to work with Agnes, I think most of my values were focused on achievement in the world. After working with her I began to realize that what really matters is that part of you, that unique individuality that is a part of you, and that is formed by your visions and your dreams and your actions and your relationship to the universe. That is how our value in the world is found. Coming back to Los Angeles, I became much more aware of how I was relating to my friends and what I was doing in terms of living in harmony with the universe rather than just eating up the universe, using it with no consciousness.

Anything else besides your values?

I think the fact that I could determine who I am as a woman, through my own perception rather than someone else's…this was a big change for me, a big healing. I now have a feeling of being centered, of knowing what I'm doing. I have a purpose and I am familiar with myself in a way that I had never been before.

One of the interesting things Agnes taught me came up when I asked her about a certain Biblical expression that kept running through my mind: "Many are called but few are chosen." She said, "Oh, that's nonsense! Everyone is called and everyone is chosen. But few of us have the courage, or are willing to take the personal power, to follow our dreams, to follow what it is to find our full potential in the world."

I have been very curious. Has all this changed your relationship with your daughter? Are there any things that are different between you now?

It has changed tremendously. When I left to go and work with Agnes, my daughter was a mirror of me, and we were very close. But now I find that I can really see into her spirit and I see places she needs to grow which I never saw before. Of course, when you begin to see your potential as a person, naturally you can help other people realize that as well.

When you talk about personal power, I can't help but reflect that there are many people who wouldn't go on a journey of the kind you describe. They just don't. So how does one work on this material… or is that a gift?

No, I don't think it's a gift. I mean I certainly do feel that a lot of people are gifted—there's no question about that. The journey to personal power comes easier to certain people than to others. I found it really interesting, I was just in

Seattle, where I was born, and I hadn't been back in twenty-five years. I saw all my friends from when I left, in my teens, and I saw that most of them had not followed their dreams. They had gotten into situations, a kind of comfort zone, and had stayed there. It was very frightening to them to hear about change—to hear about what I'd done. They really wanted to back away from that. They put it in the category of "woo-woo," you know, magic or something that was outside their experience. But it isn't outside anybody's experience to be able to work on themselves, to find that kind of dignity in their lives.

Well, it does take courage to jump over the edge and that's certainly what you did when you left Los Angeles to go to the wilds of Canada and study with a shaman woman!

Sometimes I think living in Los Angeles may be jumping over the edge.

That's a good point, that's a good point!

I think maybe I said this earlier but it has to do with understanding our personal power. Agnes repeated to me so often that women can be as powerful as men and still retain their femaleness. And she stressed that a lot with me, that women have so much to give as women and we should not blindly adopt another role, a male role. It is important that we stay feminine, stay beautiful. That is part of our power.

▲

Section Two

▼

Walking in Balance

Can you identify what it was in your life that prompted you to leave your home in Los Angeles and go to study with Agnes in the wilds of Canada?

Well, at that time in my life I was not happy. There's no question about that. I really felt that there was a lot in life that we do not see in just ordinary vision. I had spent most of my life trying to please other people, my family and so forth, and I realized that I was having a very difficult time defining who I was as a woman. I was trying to not only figure out what I didn't want to be as a woman but I was searching for what I did want. As an art dealer, which I was at the time, I was trying to find a way, a path, something that meant something to me.

I had many male teachers at that point and they had given me a great deal and I am very grateful to them. But I realized that I really needed to learn from a woman. I don't know how it all really fit together or why Agnes came into my life exactly at that time, she's never really answered that question. But surely it all started when I went down to Guatemala and met that Indian man in Tikal who told me I would receive two helpers, a man and a woman. These turned out to be Grey Wolf and then Agnes.

Lynn, we spoke earlier of your male antagonist during your study with Agnes, a person named Red Dog.

It's an extraordinary experience, and if you don't understand the world of sorcery it's hard to believe. Red Dog is a white man, a priest who came onto the reserve years ago holding up the sign of the crossed roads, which is the crucifix, saying that he was going to change these Indians' heathen ways.

It wasn't long before he realized that they were living a much more sacred life than he had ever known. In addition, he recognized that they had a lot of power. He is a man stuck in greed and fear, who wants power but only wants to use it in a very negative way. He wants to manipulate people for his own good, for his own purpose. He met a man named Twin Coyotes on the reserve. Twin Coyotes wouldn't work with him because he realized that what this man needed was his femaleness. He needed to heal the femaleness within himself. So Twin Coyotes took the man to Agnes Whistling Elk. The minute he met Agnes he realized that this woman was incredibly powerful, and he left the church at that time and went to work as her apprentice.

Agnes was very young then and felt that she could change him, that she could do something for him. What really happened is that he fell in love with her, wanted to marry her. Actually, I imagine he didn't really fall in love, he just realized that there was no way he could heal the femaleness in himself, so he schemed that by marrying Agnes he would have the power he wanted.

Of course, Agnes would have nothing to do with him as a lover or potential husband. So he stole the marriage basket, the symbol of the power of woman, which had been in her possession. And he kept the basket for quite some time. In prophecy Agnes had learned that she could not steal or take the basket back from him, though she could train an apprentice to take it back and that apprentice would be a white woman.

And you became that apprentice.

Amazingly enough!

Your encounter with Red Dog in Los Angeles...

Yes, okay. I had worked for several years with Agnes, then she told me not to return to her until I had finished my first book, which was one called *Medicine Woman*. So I was back in Los Angeles, really kind of horrified because I didn't know how I was going to write a book. Although I had always loved to write I had never had the discipline to sit down and write my own book, and of course, that is what Agnes had been teaching me, the discipline. The process of writing a book for me was to make an act of power, an act of beauty in the world that would function as a mirror for me to understand certain parts of myself. But, since she teaches experientially, she never tells you what it is that she wants you to know.

I finished writing the book, which was a monumental effort for me. And I was very proud of myself and very excited about it. I forgot about the importance of being shielded, of taking care of one's own lodge, so to speak. I was at the Beverly Hills Hotel for two days, waiting to go to Canada to be with her. I had rented out my house and had met Grey Wolf at the hotel. We had an appointment to meet some film producers from New York who were going to make my book into a film.

I was waiting outside the hotel for Grey Wolf and I saw this limousine drive up and I thought, gee it must be a politician or whoever, maybe a rock star. It was odd. The man who got out of the car was in a wheelchair. I will never forget it. I looked at him and thought there's something familiar about him. Of course, I didn't recognize him and he wheeled by me, ordering around everybody within earshot, being very obnoxious, causing kind of a scene.

He rolled right by me and brushed against me so hard that if Grey Wolf hadn't caught me I would have fallen into the flower bed. He just rolled on into the lounge and from the moment that he brushed against me I was feeling really ill. I just got real dizzy, you know, how you get when you haven't had anything to eat for a long time. Anyway, I went into the hotel and we sat down and ordered a drink, waiting for these people to come. All the time I'm sitting there I'm just really getting more and more ill. Finally, the producers arrived and I was acting very strangely. I'm sure they thought I was drunk.

During the course of just ordering a meal and drinks and so forth, there were these shining lights coming through the windows, sunlight, shafts of light coming down, and I was reminded of the end of my book, where I was taking the marriage basket back from Red Dog. There were these incredible fibers that you can see, luminous fibers that were connected to the basket, to Red Dog. When I was taking the basket I had to cut these fibers and I know that really sounds crazy but it's true. You know, you can't separate yourself from them just by cutting the physical fibers. It's an invisible web.

The whole situation in the lounge was not unlike the experience I'd had with Red Dog up in Canada...my last confrontation with him. The people at my table, the producers, were saying, "Oh, Lynn, there's no such thing as sorcery. There isn't any such thing as magic, you know, let's get down to business."

All this time I'm watching these beams of light behind their heads. I looked across the room at these little sparks of light off to one side of the room. I realized that this man in the wheelchair was sitting over there and there were these little pieces of light coming from his feet. I looked down at his feet and he was wearing moccasins with glass beads and they were glinting in the sunlight. He was wearing a pinstriped suit and I mean, I looked down at his feet. I went, "Oh my God!" Suddenly I got really sick and doubled over. There was a bead, a little turquoise bead on my leg, embedded in my calf, and it fell down, skidded across the floor, and I turned to Grey Wolf and said, "Red Dog!" Then Grey Wolf realized what had happened. His reaction was instantaneous.

At that point Red Dog just rolled out of the lounge and he was gone. In the meantime I thought I was dying. I couldn't catch my breath. I was choking. They took me upstairs and Grey Wolf put me through a ceremony and so forth. Anyway, I lived through it but for a while there I was fighting for my life, no question about it.

I always hesitate to tell this story because it sounds so incredible that a man who had become a sorcerer on an Indian reserve in Canada would show up at the Beverly Hills Hotel, of all places! But it's important to understand that a sorcerer of that kind is a master of his art and he will show up in the most unlikely places.

There are many sorcerers in this world—in business, in politics, in every walk of life. And they are always there when you least expect them. And he certainly surprised me.

What was Red Dog trying to accomplish by attacking you in that way?

I took his woman power from him, in the form of the marriage basket. I had tricked him. He was not expecting someone like me, so new to the world of power, to come after him. He just didn't expect it. And I tricked him and did take back the basket from him and he'll never forgive me for that. On the other hand, he doesn't know what to make of me. He thinks it may have been just luck that I took the basket from him. But nevertheless, I nearly destroyed him, because without woman power there is no power for a shaman man, for a sorcerer, for a magician.

When a sorcerer goes into his power he goes into the female side of himself. You know, it's interesting that C. G. Jung, the famous psychologist, talked a great deal about the anima and the animus—the feminine anima in man, and the male animus in woman.

With our shamanic teaching, we learn about the sacred twins who stand in the crack between the worlds, represented in Jung's terms as the subconscious and conscious minds. The twins can act as our translators. We are always dependent upon our dreams and visions for understanding what is in the subconscious mind. When we get in touch with the sacred twins, we discover that the anima and animus are present in all of us, it's not just the female or male counterpart. They are there waiting to be heard within each of us. Part of the shamanistic psychology I work with involves our getting in touch with those translators so that we can really understand what is in our subconscious and so that we can get a direct message and not have to interpret our dreams.

In some sense, it seems to me that Red Dog personifies that part of our culture which doesn't want to face the female side of our nature, the receptive side, the part that is hidden and that we are out of touch with. This split with the feminine has caused many of the imbalances we live with today.

Well, I think in a way he does personify that split. He also represents the dark side. We have the Virgin Mary. We do not have a Kali from India. We don't have Medusa. We don't have the dark side, and it certainly is what you choose not to look at in life that rules your life. Red Dog is the dark side.

When I first started working with Agnes she used to look at me, pat me on the head and say, "You poor dear!" And when I asked why she said this, she always replied, "Well, you have been trying to be something that you are not. You have been trying to be the Great Mother, the Nurturing Mother."

For a long time, I wasn't sure what she meant. But I slowly learned that there is the nurturing mother, the one who grows the corn, who raises the children. Even in the Judeo-Christian tradition, she's the backbone of the culture. Then there is another kind of female energy, what Agnes calls the Rainbow Mother or Ecstatic Mother, if you will. She is the one who is the poet, the writer, the philosopher, the dancer, the healer. She lives on the outer edge of society. Modern society does not support the Ecstatic Mother, the thinker and artist. So this kind of mother doesn't really feel that she ever fits in. When she gets out of college she tries to get married, perhaps, tries to live a Nurturing Mother's life. She's the one who's going to be on Valium or cocaine or is going to go mad because nobody understands what she has to give. She inspires her children instead of nurturing them. She doesn't live an ordinary schedule.

It's very, very difficult for an ecstatic woman to be married to a nurturing type man. Agnes taught me a lot about this. She taught me that for all the positive energy of the Nurturing Mother and the Rainbow Mother, there is also a negative side. Everything positive in life also has its negative aspect. For the Nurturing Mother you have a Death Mother, a Devouring Mother, on the other end of that arrow. For the Ecstatic Mother, the Rainbow Mother, you have the Teeth Mother. In every primitive society you always have masks, some way to personify the dark side. It isn't that the dark side is evil; it's just the negative side of the positive, as in photography.

If you can make a mask of the negative side, make a fetish for her, take that intangible feeling out of yourself and put it in front of you, you can light a candle for her and put flowers in front of her and say, I acknowledge your existence in the world. I acknowledge your power. Without you, without your darkness, I would not know light. But I don't want you to take me. By doing this, acknowledging her power, we free ourselves of it. It's when we choose not to look at her that madness comes into our lives.

So people with Ecstatic Mothers in their lives should light candles?

No, we should understand that she is going to inspire us in a different way than a Nurturing Mother is going to. A Nurturing Mother is going to feed us and make sure that we're comfortable and make sure we are warm and that our life is on a good schedule. The Ecstatic Mother is a different kind of energy than a nurturing type.

My own mother was a nurturing type and I am a full blown ecstatic type, and I mean to tell you that she has never quite understood me. She could never understand my leaving Los Angeles to go to the wilds of Canada. She thought I'd lost my mind. I have a child, a daughter who is a nurturing type. She was always saying to me, "Mother, can't you wear something else to the PTA meeting? Please wear something else." But now we understand how we are different. We have talked about it at great length. The same is true with my mother. We both understand that she doesn't understand me, and probably never will, but it's okay.

I think the feminist movement really needs to understand these different feminine energies—that there are women who get their greatest nourishment from homemaking, from being creative within that realm.

You mentioned that we are ruled by what we refuse to face or confront in our lives. Perhaps you could go a little further with that.

Well, particularly in this society, we don't understand the power of woman. We don't understand the importance of balance in life. We don't understand the dark side. What does that mean? When I say the dark side, many people think I mean evil. I don't mean evil necessarily. I mean negative as opposed to positive. You know, we're always taught to think positively. Look on the bright side, the Virgin Mary, God, beaming smiles. Don't complain, etcetera.

If you don't look at the dark side, you don't go through it. It's constantly there but you don't recognize it; it becomes a mystery that controls you, that takes away your power.

As a shaman, I work with people every day. When someone comes to me and I see they are denying the dark side, which almost always is the case, it invariably is being manifested as a physical illness. The dark side always manifests physically when it isn't recognized on a subtler level. For instance, I recently saw it manifest as liver disease, and at the same time on an emotional level as literally a loss of the will to live. When you have a person who is suffering from a loss of the will to live, we generally see that he or she has been ignoring subtle messages to deal with certain parts of his or her life —usually the dark parts—for years but has ignored them. Your body says, look, if you don't deal with this in this lifetime, we're going to take you into another lifetime. One way or another, you'll eventually look at it, so why not now?

You can look at someone and see where their spirit energy is leaking out. As a shaman, you can see spirit holes in people. You see that and as they work with the dark side that they've been trying to avoid you build them up in those areas. You start to go back into their lives where they have experienced the wounds that were the earliest manifestations of the dark side, with their parents and so forth.

You were talking about the feminist movement and what it has accomplished or overlooked. Let's go back to that subject for a moment.

Yes, of course. Through the feminist movement I think we've been able to realize what we don't want in life. However, it's even more difficult to decide what we do want. With two distinctly different female energies out there, it's difficult for a whole body of women to relate to just one. That's begun to change. Feminists are beginning to recognize and honor the fact that there are different kinds of female energies. You don't have to be a career woman, for example, if you are a Nurturing Mother type. And then there's another point—that there's a difference between someone's work and someone's voice. The example of Wallace Stevens comes to mind as I say this. He was a great poet and yet was the president of one of the largest insurance companies in America. Can you imagine, some of the greatest poetry of our century was written by this man in the back seat of his limousine on his way to the office! We can speculate that being the president of the insurance company was not his voice but it was his job, his way of making a living and supporting his family. His voice was the voice of his spirit, expressed in his poetry. It's important for women to make this distinction at this time. If they want to be career people perhaps that career is not their voice. It can be very difficult to put our voice and our work together, but sometimes it can happen. I've been very lucky because I'm a writer and shaman, and these are both ways that my voice is expressed.

There's a great deal of frustration for many people who are very successful in their jobs. You're getting a lot of good feelings about what you do, you feel satisfied in having accomplished something in your life. But you still have that other little piece inside you that hasn't been dealt with yet, and that's your voice. And if that's not dealt with, you're going to feel frustrated regardless of your success at your work. It's important to understand that, I think.

I'm reminded of your story and the kinds of challenges Agnes Whistling Elk put you through, many of them requiring you to face situations that were totally beyond your rational knowledge. Yet you somehow worked it out. You hung out there on the edge, sometimes over the edge.

Oh yes, sometimes way over the edge.

Most of us aren't able to do that. When we come across problems we basically try to run from them or go around them. We take the circuitous route and refuse to really jump in and mix it up. Isn't this just another case of us not wanting to deal with the darker side of our lives?

That's right. Dealing with the dark side requires us to move from a powerless place in life to a powerful one, but to do that we must face the abyss, the great void that we have to step into.

Can we switch the subject here a little? In your books you have talked about tracking, about learning how to track in the woods and what that meant in terms of your work as a shaman.

That's an interesting question. You know, a lot of people say, gee, what does what you've learned in Canada have to do with twentieth century life in Los Angeles or anywhere else? First of all, Agnes taught me that you have to be physically strong for all the spiritual work that you do. She would put me out in the wilderness and teach me how to track, how to become receptive to my prey. She taught me how to be a deer hunter, for instance. She taught me how to read tracks and know it was a doe or a buck, what time of day the tracks were made. I pulled apart the scat and could find what that animal ate. If it ate choke cherries I knew on what side of the mountain the choke cherries grew. I knew what time of day the animal moved around. I knew what time of day it went to water. I became my prey long before I ever went to hunt it, and that lesson applies to modern life in a big city. For example, if I wanted to be a radio announcer I'd track that, too. I'd learn all there was to know about radio announcing. I'd school my voice, train in electronics, do my homework. I would become receptive to that job so that when the opportunity presented itself I would be prepared. I would have lived and breathed what it was like to be what I wanted to become long before that opportunity came up. I think we don't recognize the power of this process. A lot of young people today tend to want something for nothing. They want to be president of the bank without first being even a teller. If you haven't been a teller how can you know how to run that bank? Being a teller is part of the tracking for that job.

Tracking isn't a head thing. It is something you know with your body. You know what it feels like. Agnes taught me how to follow my intuition and that's really important, very important. The intuition is the body-mind and it comes from the will. There's a whole other mind in our bodies. We're finding that the brain itself is really only a storehouse, like a computer. But the body-mind connects us with the etheric levels that are all around us, not limited by our brains or the boundaries of our physical beings.

In terms of your own life experience, what do you think your experiences up in Manitoba provided that you couldn't have gotten in the cities, say in your studies of psychology or going into therapy to better know yourself or find your personal power?

Well, you know, it's interesting. I went through Freudian analysis as a young woman. I explored many different areas of psychology. I was also very much in love with a famous psychologist, one who has made a whole new kind of psychology. Yet, through all of that, I have seen people go in and out of these processes and come out the other side knowing intellectually what they were doing, what they were about, yet never really changing. When I worked with Agnes, I changed. If I hadn't, I don't think I would have survived, truly.

When I came back to Los Angeles, I began to develop a new kind of shamanistic psychology, going back to the source, to the original nature of a person and being able to rebuild from that point. I was so changed and so much happier. I was focused and knew what I was doing with my life. I was able to put a circle of power at my own feet and not take power from someone else's circle. I think we all learn best through example and through actually living those examples out in our own lives.

When I first returned to Los Angeles, my friends recognized that I had changed. They wanted to know what had happened to me. They couldn't always relate to it, they couldn't imagine themselves leaving their families and going off to be with a shaman somewhere in the wilds, but they could see that there was something in my experiences that maybe they could learn from.

I would imagine there would have been some who thought you'd gone off the deep end.

Well, I think if any of my friends have dropped away it is because I have so little time for social things. I find that I have to stay very, very focused.

When you say stay focused and work alot what does that mean for you?

I see about four people a day—clients or apprentices or people interested in this shamanic process. And I'm writing. When I'm in L.A. I am there to work and when I am not working I am usually in New Mexico.

And why New Mexico?

Well, New Mexico is so beautiful to me. I have always loved the desert. Distance is my God, so to speak. I am close to a lot of Native people there, who are good friends of mine. Plus we have started a writer's co-op there. Stan Steiner and Scott Momaday and a group of us got together and applied for a National Endowment of the Arts grant to develop new audiences for books. So we work on that diligently.

The subtitle of your book Flight of the Seventh Moon *is* The Teaching of the Shields. *Perhaps you could talk a little bit about the shields and why they are important.*

Agnes taught me that we all come into this Earth walk like a piece of shattered mirror and each of those pieces, those fragments of our being, reflect the light of the Great Spirit. Through the process of teaching the shields, which is a process of vision, dream, ceremony and experience, you begin to fit those pieces together until finally you have a mandala, a shield that you hold up in life. The shield says, "This is who I am." The teaching of the shields is about going through that initiation, beginning in the south, in trust and innocence. In my own initiation, I had a series of dreams, a vision quest, that helped me build my shield. I took out of myself all these amorphous ideas, ideas that I really had never given form, never fully focused on. I had a lot of content and no form until I put them into a shield with symbols and objects that were powerful for me and gave me life force. Then I moved to the west and did a shield that represented the dream, death and rebirth. Then I moved to the north, to the position of strength and wisdom, and worked with the grizzly.

It's also interesting that Agnes never told you, okay, you're going to make your shield now, and this is what it's all about. First you do this, then this, and so forth...

Oh, no! As always, she puts me out there with my self, making a mirror for me to see myself. She puts me through experiences, doesn't tell me what I am doing or why. I come up with answers. The mask was the most interesting thing of all on that journey. I came to better understand the persona that we wear every day. We can have any mask we want. Yet what is underneath that mask?

One time Agnes took me out in the middle of night to look for eggs of what she called the winter bird. We walked and ran for a long, long time through the night. Finally we saw these flitting shadows across the earth. We stopped and hid behind some rocks and we watched this bird; it was the winter bird.

Agnes told me to climb high up on these rocks and get an egg from the nest without disturbing the bird. I looked and I thought, oh my God, I'll never get up there. She suddenly put this mask over my head and left me there. She said, "I'll see you back at the cabin."

I had never seen the mask before. It was made of leather and it formed to my face very quickly. After I put the mask on I found myself changing, transforming. I became whatever the mask was. It was a wolverine mask. I was suddenly fleet of foot. I went up the side of that rock and got the egg and was running like I had never run in my life. That was my first very powerful experience with masks.

One time she just left you in the cabin and said make the shield.

Oh, yes. Ruby arrived at the door and said they were going off to visit their aunts or cousins or somebody. They dressed up like two little old ladies with support hose, low heels and little pillbox hats. It scared me to death because it was so foreign. They always become the knowledge they want me to know. They never tell me what they are teaching me. Ruby is always the reflection of my fear; she scares me half to death. She can see what I'm afraid of and becomes that. In my books they change characters. Once they are like two little senile old ladies, and at other times they are wise shaman women. I think this is the most wonderful way to teach. It takes a great magician to do it because it requires much more than giving someone borrowed knowledge.

Agnes had you work with your dreams and some of them were quite extraordinary, weren't they? We all dream, yet most of us learn precious little from our dreaming process.

What you say is true. We all dream yet so few of us ever get very much from them. It goes back to the sacred twins—being able to translate from the unconscious to the conscious. In my third book, *Jaguar Woman*, Agnes worked with me through the dream state. She is a dreamer, something that is very difficult to talk about. In English we do not have words to describe the process of transformation into the spiritual. We can talk about transformation into the mental and the physical and emotional. But to talk about transformation into the spiritual, the true dream state, you just have to hold it, walk around with it, dance with it. If you describe it or try to define it, you lose the real meaning. One of the problems I've had with these books is trying to give that experience to people. I can't define it. I can only talk about my own experience. When I was sent out on a vision quest, for instance, and went into an altered state, Agnes entered into those dreams and gave me more than I probably would have had on my own. She taught me how to dream in this spiritual state. When I talk about dreams, everybody thinks of fifty different definitions for that. So let me clarify; when I talk about dreams, I am not talking about going to sleep and having a dream. In the kind of dreaming I'm talking about now, the dream takes us to other levels of consciousness, other levels that we are not ordinarily aware of. We are like radios; we can sit here and not hear the radio waves, AM or FM, coming through the room. But we know they are there because we can turn on a radio, tune it in and get hundreds of different programs coming in on those waves. It's that same way with different levels of consciousness. You have to learn how to tune that little crystal inside yourself. That doesn't completely explain it but it does give readers a metaphor to work with.

There's one last question I'd like to ask before closing this session: What advice can you give us about finding our own spiritual teachers?

A good teacher will always throw you back on yourself. A good teacher is a mirror. She helps you see you have that master within yourself. That's all a teacher does. You already know all there is to know about your own enlightenment. All you have to do is go back to the mystery, the source, the beginning of who you are. The sacred spiral, the petroglyph, that we find all around the world, in all the ancient ruins, is a symbol of birth walk. You start in the mystery, in the void, and you walk further and further away from the center, until at one point in your life you say, I want to go back to who I really am. There are all these addictions, what Agnes calls being stuck in the swamp. Your feet are stuck in mud, in all the things you believe in. That keeps you from who you really are, keeps you from going back to the source. A shamanic teacher can take you back to that original nature. It has always been my wish that my books would help people in this way. Of course, there are shamanic teachers all around the world. I think when you really want this in your life, you draw it to yourself.

So we need to ask for help?

I think so. You must make yourself receptive to your prey. If you want knowledge, wisdom, make a place for yourself, an opening inside yourself, working with femaleness, receptiveness.

▲

Section Three

▼

Earth Woman

Your book Jaguar Woman *opens as you are going back to see Agnes Whistling Elk up in Canada. It is in the middle of winter and in order to get to her place, which is in the remote wilds, you are traveling by dog sled. You arrive at her cabin and it is snowing. She's not there but you find a message she has left for you. The message tells you to go to the Butterfly Tree near the cabin. That's a good place to begin our conversation today. Tell us about the Butterfly Tree and what you found there.*

As it happens, I always follow my dreams. I'd received dreams and different signs that I should go and meet with Agnes. However, being in the dead of winter, many of my friends told me I shouldn't go, since the journey would be quite difficult. Everybody advised me not to go, and some even warned me that I would never make it. In the past, when I followed my dreams Agnes had always been there at her cabin when I arrived, so I was not worried. This time, however, after quite a trying journey, she was not there. But with the help of July, a relative of hers, I got inside her cabin and discovered her note to me, written on a piece of paper torn from a paper bag. It said she had left a gift for me at the Butterfly Tree, which in Agnes' teachings is the tree of the universe.

Agnes had shown me the Butterfly Tree during the summer and spring months. To me, it had always been an ominous presence. It frightened me. I can't explain why. It was very, very beautiful and very, very old.

The next day, July and I put on our snowshoes and set out for the Butterfly Tree. When we arrived, I could find nothing there, other than the tree. I couldn't understand what this was all about. Finally I noticed a large knothole in the trunk tree, large enough to stick your head in. So we piled up some snow and I crawled up into the tree. After slipping and sliding, I was finally able to stick my head into the hole in the trunk.

It was like stepping into another time frame, entering a time warp. It's hard to express what that was like. I had not ingested any kind of hallucinogenic but it was in many ways like what I have heard that kind of journey would be. To July, it appeared as if I was standing there for a few moments with my head in the tree. But for me it was like going on a week-long journey. First there was a whirl of colors and sounds. Out of it all the Butterfly Maiden appeared. She told me to climb to the top of the tree. If I could get to the top of the tree she would tell me something important—that was the feeling I got.

It was as though I was completely inside the tree and what I was seeing when I looked outside was the Butterfly

Tree in full bloom, covered with Monarch butterflies. As I began my journey up from branch to branch it was as if I was going through the *bardos,* from one level of consciousness to another, and through one fear after another. Instead of going into rooms where you meet your fears and conquer them bit by bit, I had to go through the center of my fears each time I entered another level of consciousness. It was as though I had to go through all the learnings of my life each time. I felt as though I was going through a pinpoint of light each time, encountering a new gateway every time I climbed from one branch to another.

It's funny. Agnes had sent me this little ally, the same one that had started me on my journey to Canada in the first place. The ally was the butterfly that I had first encountered in Santa Barbara. It kept coming to me and I realized it was trying to tell me something. So here I was inside the tree and the same butterfly, my ally, kept egging me on. It was like a little dog almost. It would jump up and down and keep me awake. At times I wanted to fall asleep, at times I wanted to just give up and fall away from the tree.

Eventually, I got to the top of the tree, up through burning branches and all kinds of fears. When I arrived, the Butterfly Maiden had taken me through my own fears. She taught me truths about my own life I had never seen before. Then she sent me on my way. I crawled back down through the tree, went through another series of fears and entered a place where I was able to see my deepest desires come to life.

I came to a juncture where I wanted to choose one way but had to go another. I fell away from the tree into the snow.

The first thing July said was, "Well, gee, did you see anything?" I couldn't reply. I didn't know what to say.

We went back to the cabin. In a little while Agnes and Ruby arrived. Nearly a week passed before I could speak about the experience. As I related my adventures to them, they told me what it meant and put it all into focus for me.

I recognized the meaning of the butterflies and I wrote about them in the book. In the real world, butterflies fly from the far north to the south; that's their normal migration pattern. The movement—from north to south—is very important. When we are on a spiritual search, we become stuck in one position or another. Using the teachings of the medicine wheel, the south is trust and innocence. If we stay in this place and don't move, we can get stuck in physicality, never gaining any knowledge or experience beyond that. Moving to the western quadrant on the medicine wheel, we encounter the sacred dream, death and rebirth, introspection. If we get stuck there, we live primarily from our emotions. Many women in our culture spend their lives in that position. We move up to the north if we're lucky, to the place of wisdom and strength and spirit. Sometimes when we move into spirit we stay there. We reject our bodies as if we didn't even exist in a physical form.

When you read *Jaguar Woman*, you'll notice that we move from the north to the south, then back to the north again. The teaching here is that in the north we have spirit but to make it work you have to manifest that spirit back into substance again, bring it back to the physicality of the south. Then, when you have substance in the south, you have to manifest that substance back into spirit, which ultimately has to do with money, with physical goods, the physical world. We were born into this physical dimension for a very good reason—to learn about the duality of life. Even though this duality does not really exist, we need to experience it before we can throw it away.

In all your books, there's the theme of fear—the importance of encountering our own fears. In Jaguar Woman *Agnes tells you that fear comes to those who create it. What does this mean—that fear comes to one who creates it?*

In *Jaguar Woman* there's a chapter called La Caldera and the Sacred Spiral, where Agnes has me experience an incredibly fearsome journey. I am sent in a spiraling fashion down through a canyon set into the floor of a jungle in the Yucatan. I am absolutely terrified to go down it because I am terrified of heights. The trail was only two feet wide, even narrower at times. Traveling was a process of going through my own fears, my addictions. I learned we often hang onto our fears like we hang onto old friends we've outgrown. In doing so we limit ourselves or even put ourselves in danger.

If we don't learn to meet them head on, our fears can become manifest in disease. We certainly choose our disease as much as we choose our joy. But most of us find it very difficult to see that we choose our fears. Agnes taught me that fears are ideas we hang onto; they are addictions. It's just like shooting up with drugs. Our fears prop us up for a while. Though it might sound like an impossible contradiction, our fears become our support system.

I seem to recall that one of your teachers said that our addictions strangle us and our fears can be addictions. They strangle the life force.

Yes, it's even more than that. When we lapse into a fear mode, we're throwing away our life energy. Fear is like an iceberg floating on the sea of enlightenment. When we live in a state of fear, we seem to be made of the same material, the ice. What happens in the shamanic process is that we melt down the iceberg that is you. You go through a shamanic death, or ego death. Ego death is the process of melting, of going from form to formlessness. The process in shamanism is often seen as the sacred spiral. We come from the mystery, from the void, from the center of the sacred spiral and we progress on our journey out into formlessness, ego death. You see this same design, this petroglyph, throughout the world, from Tibet to Egypt to the Americas. It's the mark of time. You begin at the center, the narrowest part of the spiral, and as you begin your Earth walk you get farther and farther from the center, from your original spiritual nature. Finally you are way on the outer lines of this spiral. Now, something happens in your life, a crisis of some kind, usually. And you say, I wonder what my life really means? I wonder what I am doing all of this for? So you say, I'm going to go back to my original nature. You try to walk backwards. You try and retrace your steps, tear away those veils of conditioning you've collected. But it's very difficult. It's like a cosmic joke. We come here to become enlightened; that's our purpose. Yet, it's the one thing we're most afraid of. What keeps us on the periphery is fear; fear of life, of death, fear of power or failure, fear of all the things we're afraid of.

When we start walking backwards we hit what I call these energy knots. Every time we get a little closer to the center we seem to pick up a new addiction. Each addiction puts us on the outer levels of our spiral so it becomes increasingly difficult to get to formlessness. The mind itself is a form and it makes form. We think in this society that we are mind; we believe that's what we are. Mind becomes terrified that if you succeed in your journey back to your original source, it will no longer exist. When you start talking about something irrational like thinking with the body-mind, or the power center within your body—the mind becomes frightened, just like a child. So we work with bundles and fetishes and the keeper of the mind. We let it know that it's the best tool we have in this lifetime, but we are not it, any more than we are our right hands or our little fingers.

And yet, most of the time we attach our survival to our mind!

We really do, don't we? It's a strange thing, we are mind in this society. Our attitude is, "Show me a miracle. Prove it to me. Let me see it. Let me understand it." A lot of the things we experience in shamanism, as you well know, are not exactly rational.

Lynn, some of what I've gleaned from your work is that we need to balance our lives. We need to balance the spiritual with the material. How have you brought that balance into your own life? I mean, how do you translate what you learn from a shaman in the wilds of Manitoba into the life you live in Los Angeles?

You do it carefully. It is not easy. I feel like I live with a foot in two very different worlds. But the wilderness that I experience outside of myself in Canada is part of the wilderness of my own soul. I don't lose my soul when I return to Los Angeles. I work with people on a one-to-one basis and I bring what I have learned to that work. I think it's the same for all of us. We all need to find wilderness within ourselves. We have to rediscover our instinctual nature, which we have been so very good at denying.

There is a wonderful story the shamans tell. It is told around the world because I keep hearing it from different sources. It's about a mountain lion who is about to give birth to a cub. She comes down off the mountain to find food. She finds a herd of goats and sets out to kill one of them to feed her cub. But she herself is killed in the process. In spite of her death, the cub is born. The cub is then adopted by the goats, as if it is one of their own and it grows up thinking it's a goat. It lives for a couple of years as the goats live, grazing and making noises like they make. One day a very old mountain lion, a grandfather, comes down from the forest and when he sees the young mountain lion he can't believe it. He smells this little mountain lion and he thinks, my gosh, he smells just like a goat. So the grandfather mountain lion grabs the young lion by the scruff of his neck and takes him to a river. He holds him over the river and says, "Now look at yourself and look at your reflection. You will see that you are a mountain lion like me. You're not a goat." The little lion looks and sees that, sure enough, he's not a goat after all. It's a very rude awakening for him because he realizes that he's been living life that is not real, that is not true. So he goes off with the grandfather mountain lion and learns how to hunt. Slowly, he regains his original nature.

The lesson for us is that the young mountain lion is like our repressed instinctual nature. We live like goats but we are not goats at all. We have to go out and rediscover our true nature. We are beginning to do this throughout the world. There is a new awareness of the sacredness and spirituality that we are now coming back to as we return to the center of the spiral.

Yes. Didn't Agnes tell you that in our culture, we try to avoid looking at the dark side, at our shadow?

She said that what we choose not to look at rules our lives. We look around and we see wars like Vietnam, or we see the threat of a nuclear holocaust, the actual chance that our children will never be allowed to grow up, or that none of us will be able to live on this beautiful Earth much longer. As we dare to look at all these problems, we begin to see that we ourselves have created them. The dark side, the threat of annihilation, is something we ourselves have created out of the shadow. We have created this problem. It's not just Khomeini causing a war in the Middle East. It's not just one or two or ten people out there creating these problems in the world; rather, it's each and every one of us. We're very violent people and we are choosing not to look at this in our lives. How can you not be violent if you deny the instinctual side of your own nature, or any part of your own nature? The act of denial is itself a violent act. How do we turn it around? How do we transform our violent nature? First, by looking at it and no longer choosing to deny it. Then we can learn how to master this part of our nature and use it in a creative way.

You're suggesting that as long as we're not looking at our shadow, at the dark side of our collective soul, we are being run by it. Sure! It completely dominates our lives, just as darkness defines the light in our everyday world. It's important to look at all things. In other words if you have only a positive lodestone and not a negative one, you have nothing. You have no whirlwind of fire, no spiral dance that gives life. You must have the positive and the negative. That isn't necessarily all evil and it isn't necessarily all good. We have this way of looking at life as if it has to be all black or all white. That's an incredibly unfortunate thing. As long as we cling to this way of thinking, there is no possibility for finding solutions to our present problems.

For many people who'll be reading this, I think the big question is going to be, "How can I possibly benefit from the teachings of this Native woman who is so separated from contemporary life?" How do you answer this question in your own mind, or when people at your lectures or workshops ask about it? What is it that people find in your story that they apparently do apply in their own lives?

Let me answer that in a way you might first think is a little circuitous. I once asked Agnes what she thought about the Biblical expression that says, "Many are called but few are chosen." She said, we are all called. We are all chosen. But few of us have the courage to live through what we must live through to become enlightened, to become fully realized in our human form.

Many people tell me that when I relate the story of my own journey, I offer others a chance to realize that there are alternatives to the way they are living now. There really is something we can do to change our lives, to make a positive difference and to move along the spiral to discover our true nature. We don't have to travel to Manitoba to find a native shaman woman to study with because each and every one of us has an Agnes and a Ruby and a Red Dog in our lives.

Maybe living down the block—or in our own families!

That's right. It might be your boss, a business associate, a neighbor, even one of your own children. We can always find a Red Dog in our lives. And we can find our petty tyrant, that person who pushes all our buttons. Ruby, for example, is a very scary person to me. She finds where my weak points are and she pushes on them. That's what people do in our lives. They are all teachers. If you have someone in your life that upsets you, that person is your teacher. We need to ask new questions, not "Why is this person so disagreeable!" but "Why is it that this person gets such a rise out of me? What is it in me that I need to understand, that maybe I am choosing not to look at? What is it that I am denying that is running me in this way?" And if I look at these things in a sacred way, rather than in an ego way, I begin to learn. I begin to change. I make a new choice. I start looking at what I am denying in myself and challenge my fears. Then I begin to move through them, beyond them. Again, it's the movement of the butterfly from the north to the south, then back to the north. It's the transformation of thought, the transformation of the physical in the spirit.

It's so amazing that we continue to try and close out the sacred ways, the path of wisdom. These ways seem so strange and so foreign to us...

It is interesting, isn't it? We are of this time and this soil. Yet in our search for enlightenment we travel to other continents. We go everywhere but to the United States. So here we sit, with this incredible wealth of knowledge and training, a long spiritual tradition, from the Mayans on up to the great shamanistic traditions of the north country, right here under our feet. Of course, it takes some digging to find it. After we have "conquered nature," and have all but decimated the Native cultures, the spiritual traditions that would guide us, it's no wonder it's not handed to us on a silver platter.

Our separation from the wisdom that would help us return to our true nature is supported in our language. It is interesting how language itself helps to limit what we can think and feel. For example, in English we have no words for many of the experiences associated with spiritual transformation. We have words like "spiritual" and "sacred" but what exactly do they mean? It could mean a zillion different things to a zillion different people. We even use the word "spirit" to describe intoxicating beverages!

One of the things I found particularly interesting about Agnes's teachings was when she talked about negative thoughts stealing your life force. She also talked about taking responsibility for your thoughts because thoughts are life forms.

We ourselves are thoughts that have taken life forms! But to answer your question, I find the more I work with other people the more I see a powerful tendency to feel victimized by life, by the circumstances life presents to us...

Life's doing it to me! Yes.

I work with cancer patients. So many of them are struggling with the thought that they can do nothing about their fate in life. When you tell them they have chosen their disease, when you tell them they have chosen this victim position, they get really angry. They get angry because they don't want to move off that position. It has gotten them into the problem they're in today. Choosing to change means taking responsibility for something that is almost too terrible for any of us to think about—the possibility that something we did in the past has caused a problem that can't be reversed. On one level, there's a part of them that says it is easier to continue being a victim. You have to address that part of them, and trick that part, hold up a mirror so that a stronger part of them can see what they are doing. If they can see what they are doing, then they move. The problem is, we don't want to see the ways we contribute to our own illnesses; that part of us that creates that thought form doesn't want to let go of it, doesn't want to relinquish power. Again, it's like an old friend, the product of an addiction to a negative way of thinking. It is the manifestation of an energy knot in your personality that you have chosen not to deal with. Eventually it becomes disease because the body is saying, "Look, if you're not going to learn it the easy way, then I'll disable you so that you have to deal with it. And if you still don't deal with it, then things will continue to get worse. And if you die, you die."

So the pain we experience, the disease we get, can be an expression of our unconscious. It is a way that a thought, or a pattern of thought, becomes a form.

Surely. It has to come out somewhere. But in addition to this, it's a teaching. We are here simply to learn. Our manifestation here on Earth is like a schoolhouse. We are here to become enlightened. Yet it is the one thing we're most afraid of.

Why do you think we are afraid of enlightenment?

Because the mind controls us. It does not want to lose control. Just before you go through a shamanic death, an ego death, you think you're going crazy. You might think you are physically dying. The mind is convinced it is going to physically die. But what happens is that it simply melts into the sea of enlightenment. It simply makes a shift in the way it sees the world. Everything we look at, we're really looking at it upside down. We just don't realize it. We can shift everything by realizing that what you've called reality has been a dream. You've been dreaming all along. It's like, who is dreaming who? Where does the dream originate?

You mean, like which part is the dream? Which is real?

It can be hard to tell.

Often we find out it's not so much the answers we're looking for; we're looking for the right questions to ask.

That's absolutely true. The feminist movement, for example, has been a reaction to what we *don't* want. We're now trying to decide what we really do want in the world. We're realizing the beautiful creatures women are, and the beautiful feminine qualities in men. We're recognizing the female side of life that has been so repressed and denied in all of us.

Of course, men are not these female figures. The muses of the great Rainbow Mothers stand behind the men and the children, and live through them in a way. There is a dark side of this great Nurturing Mother and that's the Death Mother. She's the snake goddess. A Nurturing Mother is usually accepted in our society. Until the past decade or so, this woman had no trouble at all. The way it usually goes, she marries her childhood sweetheart and soon after college they have children and everything is great. Then she hits forty. At that point, her children are growing up and leaving the nest. She looks around and wonders why she is still living. She doesn't understand, really. She has done everything she ever thought needed to be done, and suddenly all of that is gone. She panics. She tries to become like her Rainbow sisters, who are more the artistic type. But she doesn't know how to do that. She has to be taught. That's what the mystery schools, that's what shamanism is all about, to teach you what to do with that energy now.

Now you are going to go through the change of life which is a preparation for your real power and your real work—your spiritual work. The nurturing woman has to move her nurturing from family to the world, to animals, to whatever she finds relates to her.

Agnes teaches that there is the Rainbow Mother, however, who lives on the east of the wheel in terms of the mother energy. The Rainbow Mother is the one who never quite fits in. Rainbow Mother is the poet, the writer, the thinker, the philosopher, or the dancer. She's the one who lives on the fringes of society. She is the mad poet, the mad artist. The creative man has the muse of the Rainbow Mother standing behind him, not the Nurturing Mother. On her dark side is Crazy Woman. Crazy Woman is like a Medusa because she doesn't want to kill you, she simply wants to turn you to stone, to strip you of your abilities and your sacredness so that you can no longer function. Crazy Woman is always present in the life of Rainbow Mother. In the great Nurturing Mother, Death Mother doesn't show up too often, very seldom, not until later on in life. But Rainbow Mother battles with Crazy Woman her whole life. Always, there's a crossroads created by these four mothers. If you draw a line between the Death Mother and the great Nurturing Mother, from the north to the south, and from the east to the west, for Rainbow Mother, Crazy Mother is the crossroads at the center. That's the jaguar seat, essentially, the place of forgetting and remembering. If you sit on that seat you are riding that energy. It is like riding a horse. You hold those reins and you balance between the positive and negative. But you never want to fall over into the negative. In other words, when you look at Crazy Woman, for someone like myself, I've always been on the edge of depression. I have to be very careful not to slip over into that kind of terror. If you refuse to look at the Crazy Woman side, it gives evil a great power, tremendous power. When you see the altars down in South and Central America, you will see they are divided into four quadrants. The death side is on the left and the life side is on the right. The death side is usually much smaller than the life side because you have to balance. For everything life-giving— which you put on the right side of the altar—you must have something equally powerful to put on the left side, the death side. Death things are so powerful because we refuse to look at them. But it takes many things on the life side to balance them. When I work with a person who is a Rainbow Mother, for instance, I have her build a Crazy Woman, design her, build her, all of the things that she is afraid of. So when Crazy Woman starts to come for you, there's a certain feeling you get, the same one that great artists like Van Gogh and Cezanne felt. You have to recognize that it is Crazy Woman, pulling at you, every moment of the day and night. When you feel her coming for you, you simply put her out in an altar and light candles for her. You give her something like beautiful flowers and maybe some wine and you pray to her, you talk to her, and you look her square in the face. You tell her, I know that you are powerful. And I know that without your darkness power I would have no light. But on the other hand, I refuse to let you take me. I will not allow that. But I honor you and I honor your power.

I think of the Hindu Goddess Kali.

Absolutely! And the Hindus built temples to Kali and that's a good thing to do.

And she's very scary.

Oh absolutely! So is Crazy Woman.

As we speak, I am reminded of a great Hindu incarnation, Ramakrishna, who basically became enlightened through worshiping Kali.

That's right. It's the dark side. We have to integrate all sides of our own nature. It's not becoming the dark side but it's understanding that it's just as much a part of you as the light.

I think of how much of the dark side is expressed in the media. It's almost like that's where it comes out. It comes out in films, it comes out in television, it comes out in the news.

Yes, all of this has to do with money and control.

It's the dark side being expressed, with so little of the other side, the light side, seen.

Yes, that's true. We learn we must deal with both sides, dark and light, positive and negative. It was a great help to me to understand the difference between the Nurturing Mother and the Rainbow Mother. It freed me as nothing else. If you are a Nurturing Mother, and you fit into society, that's one thing. If you're a Rainbow Mother you never fit in. Your hard time in life is the early part of your life. You go through high school and college really wondering what's wrong with you and wondering why you don't fit in. My daughter always used to say to me: "Mother, can't you wear something different to the PTA meeting?" I'd be wearing seven veils and she'd want me to put on an Izod dress. Because she was a Nurturing Mother. I embarrassed her. I scared her. I scared my own mother because she's a Nurturing Mother. I couldn't understand why we couldn't communicate. Both my daughter and my mother are wonderful. The minute I understood that they were actually frightened, fearful that I was going to die or something—I really would forget to eat if somebody, particularly a Nurturing Mother, didn't remind me. I tend to inspire my child rather than nurture her. The Great Mother is a nurturing person. The Rainbow Mother inspires her children on ideas. My children live on ideas which are much more important than food! That's just the way the Rainbow Mother thinks.

One of the ideas that intrigued me in Jaguar Woman, *in part because of work I do in radio, was what you said about our power being in our throats. There was the idea that enlightenment is connected to one's self-expressive ability, through the voice, through the throat chakra. Could you talk a little bit about that?*

A lot of people hold their power in their throat. I find many women tend to hold power right there. They keep it closed down because they have never been allowed to express themselves. Speak only when spoken to, for heavens sake! Don't talk about wanting to be powerful. So there is always constriction there in the throat. In *Jaguar Woman*, I go down into my throat. I find symbols there and we work with those symbols.

When I first started working with Agnes, I had been through every kind of psychological process that you can imagine. I would watch people go through these different psychological systems, go through it and come out the other side and then go back to doing exactly what they were doing when they started! I had a friend who was a therapist and he worked with this very famous process for which he was known. I would say, "Well gee, if the process is so good, why is so-and-so, who is a graduate of your system, still shooting up with smack? I thought they were supposed to learn not to do that." The therapist would say to me, "Well, I have taught him to know why he does what he does. But that doesn't mean that I can change him. You cannot necessarily change people." And I said, "To me this says your process isn't working." And that's what I felt.

I'd been working with Agnes for weeks at this point, and I saw myself truly changing, I mean incredibly. I mentioned it to her. I asked her, "How come your process is working?" In effect, she said it was because the work is experiential. She told me my world was full of borrowed knowledge. She said, "You sit and talk for hours on end, and you listen to lecturers and the wonderful knowledge comes in one ear and goes out the other. You memorize it and forget it because there's no way of taking that knowledge and making it part of your own dream." She told me when I was working with her, I had to change and grow or maybe I wouldn't survive. It was often life or death. She would never say, "Lynn you need to learn how to be more disciplined." Rather, she would put me into a situation where I had to get disciplined real quick. My very survival would depend on my being disciplined. I would have to become disciplined to get out of a threatening situation, a situation where I had to face my fears.

She taught me that the sacredness is the secret, the part that makes shamanism work. She pointed out to me that many other ancient systems had included the sacred, certain truths, certain secrets, about learning how to live successfully. For example, she spoke of the pyramids of Egypt. They are symbolic, just like the medicine wheel. Essentially the pyramids represent the four cornerstones, like the four directions of the medicine wheel: trust and innocence to the south;

sacred dream, introspection to the west; spirit and knowledge to the north; and illumination to the east. She said that these four directions describe the process a mind goes through in a lifetime. That's the process of psychology. But if you don't lift up the fifth quadrant, the fifth point of the pyramid, so that you can look down on the processes of the mind from a sacred place, you could not make the process of mind work. She said that's the difference—sacredness.

Some psychoanalysts tend to be suspicious of spirit and sacredness; some are atheists. That's a problem that Jung saw, the piece that his colleagues like Sigmund Freud were leaving out.

Yeah, I think it's always useful to look behind the psychotherapist and take a look at their own life. If what they are doing is appropriate, presumably their own life should reflect it. If not, that will be there, too. It goes back to what you were saying earlier, about manifesting spirit in real life. It's not enough to know spirit and have the vision of it but what's important is manifesting it in any work where human growth is involved.

The real point may be that you don't really know any of this until you have actually manifested it in your life. We can talk a lot about it but it doesn't really exist for us, doesn't become real until we've manifested the lesson, until we are living it. That's why shamanistic work is so helpful and fascinating. We take what's intangible inside us and manifest it physically. We work with things we can touch and feel.

A while back, you were talking about the darkness and it brought me back to another idea from Jaguar Woman. *Agnes said that our culture doesn't support its artists, writers, thinkers, and poets, the people who are often expressing the darkness and the light, but expressing it in ways that are sometimes really hard to look at.*

The work of an artist or great thinker always implies change. When I was in New Mexico not long ago, I drove through a wonderful town outside Sante Fe. It was Thursday night and the low riders were driving up and down, cruising main street. I was feeling this extraordinary energy in this little town out in the middle of nowhere. I suddenly realized that it was just like shamanism—it was just like the Rainbow Mother. As the cars were driving up and down, these people were hanging onto a tradition they wanted to preserve, amongst all this other life in New Mexico. Here they were, going against the grain, swimming upstream. By going against the grain there was a very special kind of energy created. In shamanism it is the same way. In a sense, we are preserving an ancient tradition and are going against the norm. By going against the norm we create a great power. It's like Red Dog, for instance, creating a great power by creating enemies. He knows how to work that kind of energy. He understands that in creating enemies he creates power for himself. Do you see? It's going against the grain again, swimming upstream.

In the same way, Rainbow Mother and all the artists, the poets and the thinkers, are going against the grain, too. They are taking a look at life, playing the sacred clown, saying wait a minute, let's test this institution and see if it's true. The sacred clowns piss on the sacred altars. They test the priests. Let's see if this man is real, if this woman is truly a shaman. Let's find out what she's made of. It's important in a society for us to do this. Without this kind of test in a society we become weak. And it's natural that the ruling powers aren't too keen on the idea.

I look at the medicine wheel so often and I think of our society and our lives and, in particular, marriage between two people. In essence women are living in the west on the medicine wheel, while men live in the east, in the mind. They meet in the physical for an occasional encounter, then go back to their respective positions on the wheel.

Let's say two people fall in love. They move down into the south and they make love. It's a transformative experience, spiritual. For the first time, they give new life to their instinctual nature, and this pushes them up into the north, up into spirit. Then they get married because of this wonderful spiritual experience that they've had. And what happens? They start living together, start a home, and they start talking about who is going to pay the bills, and what are they going to do with the children, and who's going to work where and they start going from east to west, west to east, back and forth like a giant pendulum. They start talking about what I feel about what you think, and what I think about what you feel. Occasionally they work hard at their relationship and manage to make love in the south. What's left out, of course, is the instinctual nature, the ecstatic experience that takes them up into the north, up into spirit. What is left out of most lives is the north, spirit. When you go east, west, east, west, back and forth, our traditional psychology, there is a kind of understanding. But that's all you get. You cannot transform when you're going back and forth, from east to west and back again to east. The only way you can transform is by going south to north, north to south. You can only do that by using your instinctual nature, the mountain lion within us that we've tried to deny, or make into a goat. So how do we bring all this back into our lives to live a more total experience?

Good question!

If you are a Rainbow person, an artist, you have to find a mate that you can work with in some way. It doesn't mean that you both have to be painters. But somehow you need to have a common goal, a common ground that you truly work at. Not just an idea or symbolism that you're working towards, like, we both want to have a happy spiritual life. But something that you're really putting effort into every day. When you are a Nurturing Mother, or when you have two nurturing people, their children really are their spiritual endeavor in a way. But with Rainbow people, they have to be careful of that. They meet someone and they are ecstatic about them. They move right up into the north, but then they get married and they get caught in that east-west journey. They get lost in it and they don't understand what's happened, why the magic has gone out of their relationship.

How do you maintain the magic in the relationship?

By truly working together, by consciously manifesting substance into spirit and spirit back into substance. It has to be done or you lose one another.

I think there's something in our culture that teaches us that there's something not quite right about male and female working together. It's a no-no. You don't want to do that.

After all, how can you spend all that time together? How boring! This is not to say that it can't be done, not at all. We can work together and manifest in a conscious and creative way. The sacred wheel can help, if we'll just look at it. Look at what we're doing, at how it looks on the wheel, and then keep the wheel moving in our lives. Maybe you look at each other and say, "We've been living east-west for three weeks now. How about a little north-south movement?" And that's the challenge, isn't it?

▲

Section Four

▼

We Are All Shamans

Lynn, you have written that we are all shamans, that each of us has the capacity to make use of sacred rituals and do shape shifting, just as shamans did centuries ago. You say that deep down inside us is a longing for the wilderness, for access to spirit and the power of other realities, but most of us have become quite separated from our instinctual natures and know little about this world you speak of. Still, we do encounter our magical powers when we travel through the inner space of our dreams and imagination, or when we witness a baby being born, or when we watch a flower bloom or find new universes contained in the workings of a single atom. But how do we access the power we feel all around us, the power hidden in all the mysterious corners of our world? You talk about how we choose borrowed knowledge above our own, subverting the power of real discovery. You say that as shamans of this age, our task is to heal Mother Earth, but we cannot do this until we have first discovered how to heal ourselves. I wonder if you could clarify some of the issues you bring up here. How do you see shamanism? What is it to you? How can each one of us take a more active part in the world you describe in your books and lectures and workshops?

Shamanism is a way to create bridges between the everyday material or physical world and the world of spirit. Shamans have lived through a life-threatening situation and have come out the other side with special capabilities or a special vision of what our lives are all about. In contemporary life, there are millions of people who have done extensive inner work on themselves, and are shamans in their own right. They are people who have lived through disruptive family lives, people who were beaten up, either emotionally or physically, people who have learned to survive in an alien world and discover realities invisible to most of us. When you look at the history of shamanism in ancient times, shamans were often people who had near-death experiences, or faced madness, only to come out the other side with the ability to perceive realities other than those most of us know, realities that some say exist in parallel to everyday existence.

I think most of us have come to associate shamanism with native cultures, the image of the medicine man or the witch who was able to foretell the future, heal people, perform sacred ceremonies. You're kind of enlarging on that definition here, aren't you?

Let's not forget that the term "shaman" was actually invented by anthropologists, not by the Native peoples themselves. We have few words in English to describe the spiritual life of the shaman. Any society is reflected in the language they speak. It is important to recognize how difficult it is for us to even be able to talk about the sacred world of the shaman. Our language is one of a very material society that has little room for concepts such as the evolution of the spirit or enlightenment.

My own teachers happen to be shamans. I also have been called a shaman, a shaman of the twentieth century. I work with the harmonies of Mother Earth, with primal instincts. Those who are my teachers speak of choreographing the energies of the universe through the instrument of this body, this magnificent body that we have.

And so your belief is that all of us have this potential. We might not manifest it at this moment but we all have this potential.

Yes, that's true. You know, when I first met my teacher, Agnes Whistling Elk, I had been dreaming about her for three or four months, night after night. I will never forget that evening when I knocked on the door of her little cabin in the middle of the Canadian wilderness, the woman who answered was the woman I'd been dreaming about night after night. I was stunned. I knew instantly that I had indeed found my teacher. I sat down at her wooden table in the middle of her room and she proceeded to tell me things only I knew about myself. I had come in search of the marriage basket that I'd seen in that photograph in the art gallery. And she went on to tell me that the marriage basket was woven from the dreams of all women and that it was a very sacred object and symbol in their world. She made it clear to me that I had come into a place of teaching and learning that I had asked for but did not understand: "You've made a bid for power and it has been answered, if you so choose," she said.

I asked her, but why me? I had been living a fairly ordinary life in Los Angeles—if you can live an ordinary life in Los Angeles. I had just come out of a difficult marriage. I had a daughter and was looking at my life and thinking that there had to be more than what I'd been seeing. I thought I had nothing to prepare me for the world Agnes was making available to me. If somebody had told me I would be sitting here with you, talking about these extraordinary events that I've experienced these past few years, I would have just laughed.

Your work and your books have been compared to those of Carlos Castaneda. How do you see that comparison?

I find this fascinating because Carlos calls himself a sorcerer, which often has negative connotations, though as I understand it sorcery need not be negative. On the contrary! Carlos works with the world of personal power and he's learning about that world as a man. I am a woman, and my teacher is a woman. I have written my books exactly as I have experienced the realities that have been shown to me. The teaching is a female teaching, I believe. It's useful to men who are trying to understand their female side, or their female shield. But it is female centered.

In terms of Castaneda, I think our worlds are quite different because I teach people to heal the mind and the heart. Yes, that does involve personal power but I think it's used very differently. The way of teaching, however, focused on shamanic understanding of energy, is pretty much the same throughout the world, throughout any of the shamanic teaching situations that people find themselves in. You have a teacher and you have another person over here who is always moving your energy around. Ruby Plenty Chiefs plays that part in my teaching process. She's the one—when I get too serious or too self-centered, too obsessed with an idea, or start taking myself too seriously—she is the one who always moves me out of that place, either exercising her ability to terrify me or make me laugh or to bumble in some way that is confounding.

In the case of Castaneda's work there has been a great deal of controversy as to whether it's true or not, fiction or non-fiction. There has been similar controversy over your work. How do you deal with criticism of this type?

When I brought my first book, *Medicine Woman*, to an agent, that I thought might be able to sell it to a publisher for me, I very carefully told her this was something I had experienced. It was autobiographical. Two or three weeks later, I went back to talk with her. When I walked into the office a gentleman was standing there with her and she proceeded to tell me that the book could never be sold the way it was. She said it was badly written, nobody would believe it. She told me this man here could rewrite my book and then maybe we would have the possibility of selling it.

I was horrified because I had specifically told her this was a book about my experiences. I could not change what I had lived through. So I took my manuscript and left.

Incidentally, she came to me years later and admitted how wrong she had been. She said she wished she had paid the manuscript the attention she now realized it deserved. The lesson here is that people find it difficult to believe something they have not experienced for themselves. And I can't criticize that. In fact, I always tell people you shouldn't believe something you haven't experienced. One of the first things Agnes ever told me was that we live in a world of borrowed knowledge. We sit and we listen to other people pontificate about their experiences but there comes a moment when we must somehow make that experience part of our own dream. If it's borrowed knowledge, if it isn't part of our experience, how do you do that? Right in the beginning, with my teachers, it became very clear that what they were going to teach me I had to live through. Often there were situations where I had to significantly change who I was in order to survive—literally change the way I perceived a situation in my own reality. What that taught me was how to take command of my own life. Most of my work is about that. It's about taking your power, taking command of the realities that you have created but often don't accept as your own. As a result, when people talk to me about my books they say, my golly, you've lived through such an extraordinary scenario. You know, why all the drama? Why can't this just be simple? Why can't enlightenment just come easily? I think sometimes it can, depending on the person and depending on what it is you're trying to learn. But if you're trying to get over, say, an abusive background, a co-dependency issue, addictions, these struggles are not going to be easy. It is difficult to change the conditioning that we've had. There is just no question about it. Enlightenment is sometimes joyous and sometimes very painful. When I look at how I illustrate that in my books, through my own experiences, it seems that I am a person who needs a lot of drama to learn. I'm sure other people don't necessarily need that but I'm only writing about me. If somebody had told me years ago what I was going to experience in *Windhorse Woman,* in Tibet, I would have said you're crazy, there is no way in the entire world that, first of all, I am going to risk my life by sneaking across the border into Tibet in the middle of the night and so on. I just wouldn't have believed it.

Some people say they would find it easier to believe my experiences if they were about a man. They find it easier to believe that a man could do what I have done. It is less acceptable coming from a woman. I really don't know how to answer your question any better than that—that most of my critics have simply never experienced anything like this, and they don't find it easy to believe that anyone else could either, least of all a woman. But any of the experiences I write about are right on the edge of our daily perceptions if we will open our magical eyes and see.

We are extraordinary instruments, but so many of us use such a tiny portion of our brains, such a tiny proportion of our abilities. I often think about the time that I brought a radio to aboriginal friends of mine in Australia. They'd never seen such a thing. They'd not been touched by the outside world. I brought it to them because I wanted them to laugh. I knew that it would bring a great joy to them. And it did.

I set this thing down in the middle of the hut and explained that it would bring in sounds and voices whose source they could not see. We talked about a ceremony we had done the night before in sacred dream time, about moving into dream time and meeting all these extraordinary beings. Then I turned the radio on and all of a sudden

Beethoven's Fifth Symphony filled the hut and they were filled with awe. They were so excited! They laughed and we talked about it, with the men and women of power that were in that village, for a long time.

I realized that is like us. We have this instrument, the human body, but so many of us do not know how to turn it on and tune it in. We don't know how to tune into the magnificence of this universe, and we even avoid trying. To discard all that, before you even know it, is to me a great tragedy.

It reminds me of the great Joni Mitchell song from the sixties: "Turn Your Radio On."

Yes! Yes! I like that!

It occurs to me that this certainly is a time for the emerging power of women. In fact 1992 was called the Year of the Woman because so many women came into the political process. It also occurs to me that there are a lot of women finding their power, and it has brought them a lot of criticism.

I think there are dialectical waves of power, the ascending and receding power of both men and women. Throughout the history of the world, it has gone in cycles or waves. My teachers have said that before the patriarch on this Earth, there was a matriarch. They have said that the Earth is indeed a school house, and that we have all been here before, whether we remember it or not. One of the things we are learning is about male and female power, how they are different, and perhaps that is why we see one kind of power dominating for a while, only to cycle back to the other at some time in the future.

It has been my experience that we come here to learn and understand and elevate the spirit in one way or another, be it around the gender issues or something else. Certainly my book *Shakkai* is about that. It has to do with understanding the process of time and lifetimes so that we can begin to see death and life differently. If you are afraid of death you are not going to live fully. I began to be guided beyond these experiences of past and future lives—my book, *Woman of Wyyrd*, being about past lifetimes. You begin to see that the spirit is never born and never dies. It is a continuum of energy and a reflection of the Great Spirit. This continuation of spirit is imprinted in every lifetime and with every learning journey we make back to Earth.

In your book The Woman of Wyyrd, *you dealt with a previous life in medieval times, and in* Shakkai *you deal with a future life in Japan, in the twenty-first century. In those books, you use a technique called double dreaming to realize what happened in these lives. Could you talk about double dreaming and its value?*

Double dreaming is similar to a regression into a past life but it is so much more than that, really. I have always been very leery of talking about past and future lives because I had never experienced them—not really. I had an occasional sense of things, flashes of things, but you never know what is your imagination and what you're simply wanting to be true. The dream lodge experience that I portray in both *Shakkai* and *Woman of Wyrrd* are about going deep, deep into what is almost a death-like trance. You move out of not only the physical world and the astral world, but into the etheric levels. Here it gets difficult to explain. All I can say is that it is like being right here, going into trance and suddenly walking into a movie that's already in progress. It's not like there is a beginning and a visible end. With *The Woman of Wyrrd*, I was walking down a road and I didn't remember Lynn until much later, when a few little flashes happened. After months of traveling back and forth through what we call time, it became very difficult to get back to this life. I would never suggest trying to go into double dreaming without a teacher with you because it is an ability that demands careful preparation and focus. Several times Agnes and Ruby had to submerge me in ice cold water to get me back. It is not unusual for someone to die because they can't get back to their physical body. There is something they call the silver cord, which you can sometimes actually see in the process of double dreaming. It brings you back if it's not your time.

That's the cord that has been mentioned in out-of-body travel. It reminds me of one of the early Seth books, maybe Seth Speaks, *written by Jane Roberts. Seth was talking about reincarnation and he said we don't really understand reincarnation or past lives, it has more to do with living simultaneous lives.*

That's right! Did he say that? Well, I would say it is true from what I've experienced. Agnes explained it as being like layers of a cake. You feel like you are moving through layers of energy and they look like fog, or a mesh, a series of veils. Some are tightly meshed and some are not. All of a sudden you fall into something that is moving energy and it's there and you're in it.

Maybe it's your intent to drop into this place, and maybe it's not. To be able to do this with intent, you have to develop the shaman will. That's how we move after death. You move with your intent in other lifetimes, so the shaman will needs to be highly developed.

Do you need a teacher to do this?

Yes. I can't imagine doing it without a teacher, a guide. While I'm fairly well developed in this area, having devoted a great portion of my life to this study, I could never have done it without Agnes and Ruby.

To go back a bit in our conversation, I'm reminded of what Buddha said—something like, don't do it because I say it, do it because you find out it's true or real for you.

Absolutely!

Yet in our society, we are bombarded with the kind of thinking that says, if I can't touch it, feel it, see it, measure and quantify it, it isn't real. It doesn't exist.

That's right. We speak a pragmatic language. In German there are sixty words for mind. We have a lack of subtlety in our expression, in our words. Besides that, we don't even make use of the vocabulary we have.

I think in Tibetan there are over a hundred words for states of consciousness.

How do we even describe these states of consciousness in English? How do we think about something for which we can find no words, or when we look at our language and think, well, since there aren't words to talk about it, maybe it doesn't exist. A society grows out of the language it speaks. We speak a pragmatic language with few words for spirit.

It is certainly true we can't talk about these things if the only words we have are things like "waking," "dreaming," "sleeping"...

But we can begin to break through some of these limitations imposed on us by our language by simply recognizing that this is the problem. In *Crystal Woman* Ruby did a wonderful thing with me. I was making a sand painting. I had worked days and days on it, gathering the color and so forth. I was in a "whirly," which is similar to a sweat lodge, set against the wind. One morning Ruby came in and walked right through the center of my sand painting, casting sand to the four directions. I was furious, just furious with her. Then she asked me, "Where is the unknown? Where have you represented the unknown?" I said, "What do you mean? I haven't represented it." And she said, "Well, then there is no magic and no power in your sand painting, because power and magic comes from the unknown, from that place that is indescribable, that exquisite space that you cannot convey to someone who so desperately needs to hear about it."

She taught me that you have to take someone into the center of a powerful experience by circling it. You can only circle the truth and the sacredness of a moment. If that person has the intent and the will, they will move into the center of that sacred circle and will see that truth with their own eyes. But to describe that truth would be to lose it.

Remember that event, I think it occurred in 1991 in San Francisco, where the Tibetan monks were doing the sand painting of the

Kalachakra Mandala at the de Young Museum and a woman jumped over the rail and proceeded to mess up the sand painting that they had been working on for three weeks. It got national media attention because of the reaction of the monks. They simply allowed it to happen, and weren't upset. It didn't seem to bother them. It just seemed to be part of what was happening and so the next day they went back to recreating their sand painting, just as if nothing had happened. I think that the attention it got was because of their reaction, which certainly wasn't the usual thing of getting furious because we've been working so hard on this damn thing. There was a lesson in this that so many of us found so difficult to grasp—a sense of living in balance, of responding to the present without letting something that had happened even moments before throw us off center...

Yes. I think of something that happened in my own life about three years ago, a horrible blow. My entire family very suddenly passed away from various tragic illnesses. My first reaction was to die with them. Then I realized that you must smooth the sands of time and go on.

One Christmas we are all there, celebrating the holidays together. The next Christmas, the only ones left were my daughter and I. And to deal with that, even with all I have experienced, I had to face my mortality, and the immortality we all are, in equal measure. I had to try to understand the specter of death. It was out of that learning that *Shakkai, Woman of the Sacred Garden,* came. I was trying to find that place of peace and serenity and tranquility of my own spirit.

Shakkai is this magnificent old woman-teacher, who came out of Shintoism and Taoism, and heaven knows what other magnificent teachings. She had constructed this garden, this physical garden, which I then learned how to construct myself—understanding the placement of stones and water and trees and color and knowing how it all relates to the sacred balance of Mother Earth.

But then I began to see that this is a teaching of the interior self and that finding the so-called "isles of the immortals" is really a process of making oneself understand the sacredness of the small, moving into a pinpoint, into the size of a thumb, so that you can go inside the sacred gourd, and pray there and live within the universe that is born out of that smallness. In other words, going into the atom, into the seed to find the wisdom that is planted there. Out of this teaching I began to look at death differently. I began to see that in a sense, we put on a body like a suit of clothes, and to do this becomes a tremendous teaching of duality. In the beginning, with the first lesson of power, we believe we are all alone. You have to completely own that teaching, become it, understand the duality of this existence, of the relative world of time-space that you are there and I am here. Then you move through the teachings to the last lesson of power—where we learn that we are indeed all one. There is no separation between any aspect of life.

So many people have remarked that death is a great teacher.

Yes.

And we don't really understand that until we are faced with it, either with a loved one, a family member or our own mortality, not to mention the power of having a life-threatening illness that really brings you directly in touch with mortality. I think as we get older we move into another phase in our life, where we're kind of on the down side instead of on the up side—it changes one's whole perception of life.

I think in the face of crisis we grow, we often change because we have to. The crisis in the world today, ecologically and economically, is forcing people to wake up and realize that they are destroying this planet almost as quickly as they are breathing. Clearly, we have to change. We have to change the way we live, the way we see reality and sacredness and technology. You know, Michael, I think of people going out into the world with this phenomenal technology that we have at our fingertips. To me, at our present level of spiritual maturity, it's almost like a child being given a sharp sword, or a gun, and told to go out and play with it on the playground. If you don't have the balance of the sacred within you own spirit, whatever sacred means to you, if you don't balance all of this technology with an understanding of why and where, the meaning, the deeper meaning of life, it is truly lethal, I think. It is virtually suicidal.

Let me read something you wrote: "Many people enjoy living on the edge. They dwell in the world of becoming and never completely accomplish, not really. They never truly become." Can you expand on that?

For the last several decades we've done a lot of implosion of energy, looking within for the problem, the source of problems. At some point, like mimicking the dance of life that is within each cell of your body, there has to be an implosion of energy, which is negative or female and an explosion of energy, which is male and positive. This implosion and explosion creates the sacred spiral, the dance of life. We have not done a lot of exploding into the world with ceremony, with a celebration of what we have learned in all of these years of introspection. We are always becoming, and what that means is that we are always *recovering;* we are never *recovered.* This is not to say that we ever stop learning. That's a process that's ongoing for all your life. But there are rites of passage along the way. There are plateaus where you need to rest—where you need to say, okay, this is what I have done up until now and isn't it fantastic that I have been able to do and accomplish what I have done. And people say, well, what if you're talking to someone who has never accomplished anything? I think that anybody who is even surviving in the world of today has accomplished something.

This "becoming" idea is intriguing and it reminds me, as you talk, of a book I read some years ago about Crazy Horse and Custer, two contemporaries of history. Both were leaders of their people. Both also died at a young age, were killed, and both became mythic figures. The difference between Crazy Horse and Custer was that Custer was always working on becoming something else. In fact, there's a theory that he was really trying to become the presidential nominee when he went to Little Big Horn. By contrast, Crazy Horse could not even conceive of the idea of "becoming"—he was interested in "being". To me, this is an excellent example of what you are talking about, the concept that we are always becoming something, moving toward the future, but that we don't understand very much about what it is to just be.

We believe we are not good enough when we are just being.

And we're not simply content to be in the moment with what is. We're always kind of going for something else that is beyond our reach.

Agnes asked me one time, "Lynn, what have you gained from this work of ours together?" And I said, "Well, I have become a healer, I've become an author, I've become a teacher." Agnes was glowering at me, and she said, "No, you are a woman living your medicine, who happens to write, who happens to teach." I was so taken aback. I thought about that for a long time and that's when I came to those ideas, that we are always becoming instead of just being. It's very difficult in this society, with so much emphasis placed on becoming something. You know, and I do talk a lot about acts of power—not because of what you become but because of the teacher, the mirror that is created through a focused effort. Being within the process of what and who you are is important, has to be done, but that's not the process of celebration. No matter who or what you are! No matter who you have become! You have to own that and sit on that plateau of real celebration of who you are. You have to center yourself on that plateau of your being before you can move on, with a kind of newly established energy.

Something else you've written about, since we're talking about power, is the hoops of power. What are the hoops of power?

The hoops of power are sometimes talked about as rings of power. They are interpreted differently by different people. We talk about hoops of energy and power as being hoops of energy that kind of fit one on top of another. It's not an up the ladder club, it's just a matter of being equal distance from the center. When we first come into life, we are in the first hoop of power; we're learning to navigate through this dimension. There are certain things like an act of power that kind of catapults you through this kind of cloud layer that a lot of people experience in their lives. They can never get up past that layer, a lid that keeps them down, so to speak. I've heard so many people describe it to me in that way—as a lid. The act of power, as I have come to understand and teach it, is not power over something, or power over other people, but having the ability and the passion and the accessibility to your own passion so that you can manifest your dreams in the world. When you do that, when you focus your energy in that way, you then become conscious of the shaman within you, that medicine person, that power woman, whoever that is, that enables you to begin to take control of your life. I don't mean control in the manipulative sense, I mean being able to understand that you create the reality that you live in.

You mention in Shakkai *that our emotions control our lives and keep us from the mysteries of life. What do you mean by that?*

If our emotions are negative, full of fear, for instance, if we're afraid we'll not be liked, that's a disease. We want to do what is right, what will gain us positive attention from others, which is a wonderful idea, in a way. But it should not be at the expense of our own integrity.

Emotions are very important when you are doing ceremony. To become a warrior of the spirit you have to understand emotion. But understanding emotion has to do with being able to contain emotion in a way that is forceful. Holding emotion like a woman in menopause holds her blood— she then becomes a wise woman—she's holding her power. You learn to hold your emotions in the sacred gourd of your being, only to be expressed in a positive way that is full of light. But this should not be confused with being Pollyanna-ish, either. Emotions can keep us from the mysteries of life because of terror, because of what is new, what is changing in our lives. We find the terror of—Oh, my gosh, I'm no longer in control!—that sort of thing. Well, in actuality, I don't know that we ever are in control. But standing in the integrity of your own truth—that's a different kind of control. Emotions have tremendous power. When you think of it, it is this power that is responsible for all the wars on this earth. We are absolutely irresponsible about our thought forms and those thought forms are reality. They exist as energy forms and we need to look at how these forms, which we create, are affecting the universe around us. What is it that allows us to be so blind to how the emotions we create affect the world around us—other people as well as the physical environment. I think that blindness must come from that feeling of duality, the illusion that we are all alone. We don't understand that we merge into and interact with other energy forms every day at every moment.

So the power of negative emotions can be destructive to us.

Absolutely. A lot of the fear that generates these negative emotions comes from the fact that we don't tune in to the instinctual side of our nature. We deny such huge pieces of ourselves, having to live in urban societies, living on top of one another. You can't live like a wild animal, a wild thing racing through the streets; you have to "control yourself." And in that process you deny the wildness that is you. That wildness comes out in the work I do in shamanism. We work with power animals, we work with those aspects of ourselves that are very, very, real. But because as a people we deny the animal kingdom, we feel the animal only as a beast that does not have an intelligence or any kind of spirit, any kind of valuable life, we deny the animalistic part of ourselves.

In wildness is the preservation of the world.

Amen!

Isn't this another illustration of our living in our heads, of failing to live in our hearts, or at least get a balance between our head and our heart—again, this society, I think, conditions us to do that.

We live in our heads and don't know how to access the power of the heart and the power of emotion, the heartfelt emotion. In my work, I often see people move out of their heads and into their power centers around their navels, or into their hearts, and all of a sudden they become very strong. When you are centered in your head somebody can physically push you over very easily, for instance. You are out of balance. Not only with your physicalness but with the energy of the universe around you and in you. It's an ancient art to move your energy and your thought forms down into the "chi," the center around your navel area. And it's easily demonstrable to people who don't understand that, who feel that can't possibly be true, that we are mind, in a sense. We identify with mind and mind is a magnificent, powerful tool but it is also limited.

Something else you talked about in many of your books is the idea that one needs to honor the dark side or be ruled by it. Could you briefly elaborate on that?

It's what we deny in life that rules our lives. If you deny the aspects of yourself that torment you, that come up in the hidden terrors in the middle of the night, those places within yourself that you refuse to look at will absolutely move into your life and take over. We seem to have a society that makes a lot of affirmations. These can be very good, you know—positive thoughts. But to make positive thoughts you have to understand that there is always a double-edged sword, there is a positive side, there is a negative. That somewhere, darkness does define the light.

It's like, we want to hide the homeless and the hungry, who are, some have said, manifestations of our shadow, of our dark side.

That's right. Hide the fact that there is torment and grief, hunger and tremendous violence—and deny that we are all responsible for creating it because there isn't any one of us who doesn't have secret corners within us that we are afraid to look at. Eventually it comes out in the form of disease in the body. Or poverty in our culture. If you have a disease in the body there is something that you're not looking at, and if you are a spiritual person, you take advantage of that teaching and you say okay, obviously I haven't been paying attention. What is it, body, that you are trying to teach me? And you can learn about that through symbolism. In *Shakkai* I talk a lot about that, about the symbolism of the body. If your stomach is hurting badly and you begin to have an ulcer, maybe it means there is something you can't "stomach" in your life. And that sounds very simplistic but it is so often true. I've worked with too many people in the process of going to the source of their dis-ease. It is absolutely so important for people to realize that—that this body is not something to be thrown away in the spiritual process but something to be honored, that it is a magnificent temple of the spirit and we've chosen it for a reason, with all of its frailties as well. Because those frailties provide a mirror that you cannot avoid looking into. You can have teachers all over the place. You can avoid the things that make you a little uncomfortable. You can just look away. But your body lives with you and mirrors back all of who you are.

What about finding your sound?

My first experience with sacred sound was being submerged in a pool with my teachers. They had me make a tone and I found that there were tones that resonated with me and there were those that didn't. The ones I resonated with fed my spirit. I loved them. I became almost obsessed with them. And that was the beginning of a teaching around the sacred sounds. There was something similar called the *kotodama,* in the Orient. Incidentally, in all my writings the words are woven together a certain way so that the sacred sounds form an invisible fabric and harmonic throughout. This provides a way of not only seeing the words but hearing them as well. They move into the subconscious in a way that is enlightening and helps you expand towards higher knowledge.

So, how does one discover one's sound?

Well, you can do it in your bathtub. Submerge about half way. You don't submerge all the way. And darken the room, light a candle. Then slowly go up and down the chromatic scale with your voice. You will find a tone you resonate with.

When this happens, you will find that it will make you feel wonderful. There are other sounds that you absolutely can't stand. Find an instrument, maybe a chime or tuning fork, that will make the tone you like. Sound it throughout the day, at different times, and you will find that it can actually heal you when you are feeling out of balance. In a sense, sound holds the world together.

The sound has power.

Oh, tremendous power. I was told by one of my teachers in the Mayan land, during the writing of the book *Jaguar Woman*, that great objects like the pyramid can actually be moved with the use of sound. I am told that in ancient history that is one of the powers they used. In one ancient legend that Agnes has often told to me, sound holds the world together, and, as I am beginning to see, there is a great truth to that. So then you might wonder, what happens when you are in New York City and you hear the cacophony of sound of horns and yelling and screaming. What does that do to the process of life?

Yeah, and what does it do when you walk in the woods and feel the sounds of nature around you? It's very different.

Yes, a very different kind of sound. And that sound of nature, or the sound which resonates for us, is healing if we allow it. You know, if you are filled with emotions that are disparate and full of fear, negativity, envy and jealousy, you will miss it all, you know. You will not hear the sound.

If you will allow your emotions to float through you, and you don't hang onto them like a possession, if you just let them go and kind of watch them move through, then you begin to experience the sacred witness. And it is that sacred witness, in the last analysis, that is all you really are.

Biographical Notes on Michael Toms

Michael Toms is recognized as one of the leading spokespersons of "new paradigm" thinking. His perspective has been influenced greatly by his work with the late Joseph Campbell and Buckminster Fuller. He is perhaps best known as the host and executive producer of the widely acclaimed and award-winning "New Dimensions" national public radio interview series. He is Chairman Emeritus of the California Institute of Integral Studies, and currently serves as Senior Acquisitions Editor with HarperCollins San Francisco. His previous books include the bestselling *An Open Life: Joseph Campbell in Conversation with Michael Toms* and *At the Leading Edge: New Visions of Science, Spirituality and Society.* His interviews with leading thinkers of our time are the subject of our extensive "New Dimensions Books" series, edited by Hal Zina Bennett.

About New Dimensions

Inspired by the need for an overview of the dramatic cultural shifts and changing human values occurring on a planetary scale, New Dimensions Foundation was conceived and founded in March 1973, as a public, nonprofit educational organization. Shortly thereafter, New Dimensions Radio began producing programming for broadcast in northern California. Since then, more than 4,000 broadcast hours of programming intended to empower and enlighten have been produced. In 1980, "New Dimensions" went national via satellite as a weekly one-hour, in-depth interview series. More than 300 stations have aired the series since its inception, and "New Dimensions" has reached literally millions of listeners with its upbeat, practical, and provocative views of life and the human spirit.

Widely acclaimed as a unique and professional production, New Dimensions radio programming has featured hundreds of leading thinkers, creative artists, scientists and cultural and social innovators of our time in far-ranging dialogues covering the major issues of this era. The interviews from which this book was compiled are representative.

As interviewer and host, Michael Toms brings a broad background of knowledge and expertise to the "New Dimensions" microphone. His sensitive and engaging interviewing style as well as his own intellect and breadth of interest have been acclaimed by listeners and guests alike.

New Dimensions Radio provides a new model for exploring ideas in a spirit of open dialogue. Programs are produced to include the listener as an active participant as well as respecting the listener's intelligence and capacity for thoughtful choice. The programs are alive with dynamic spontaneity. "New Dimensions" programming celebrates life and the human spirit, while challenging the mind to open to fresh possibilities. We invite your participation with us in the ultimate human adventure—the quest for wisdom and the inexpressible.

For a free *New Dimensions Journal,* including a list of radio stations currently broadcasting the "New Dimensions" radio series, or an audio tape catalog, please write New Dimensions Radio, Dept. AB, P.O. Box 410510, San Francisco, CA 94141-0510; or you may telephone (415) 563-8899.

New Dimensions Tapes with Lynn Andrews

Medicine Woman with Lynn Andrews

This conversation includes the nether regions of sorcery and power. Lynn tells of her extraordinary spiritual journey as an apprentice to the North American Indian medicine woman Agnes Whistling Elk. She talks about the marriage basket, which is a symbol of the warrioress within, and how our beliefs become barriers to consciousness. We limit ourselves by what we think we believe.
Tape #1643 1 hr. $9.95

Walking In Balance with Lynn Andrews

Provocative and poignant, this conversation traverses the path of the Indian Medicine Way as Andrews relates her extraordinary adventures as an apprentice to a Cree medicine woman in Manitoba, Canada. Recovering the femaleness of our nature and facing our fears are the twin bridges to wholeness within. Dream visions, teaching of the shields, the way of the Rainbow Warrior and more light up the landscape of Andrews' mythical and mystical quest. She is the author of *Medicine Woman* (Harper & Row 1981) and *Flight of the Seventh Moon* (Harper & Row 1984).
Tape #1859 1 hr. $9.95

Earthwoman with Lynn Andrews

This is a remarkable visit with Andrews, who speaks of her apprenticeship to a Native American shamaness, Agnes Whistling Elk, and how her extraordinary journey into the unknown leads to dazzling new worlds of the mind and spirit. She speaks of reclaiming her personal power as a woman and at the same time opens up ways for everyone to tap the hidden powers of their own nature. Through a wealth of practical shamanistic lore interwoven with tales of sorcery, Andrews reveals both the challenge and the rewards of the sacred quest. She is the author of *Medicine Woman* (Harper & Row 1981) and *Jaguar Woman and the Wisdom of the Butterfly Tree* (Harper & Row 1985).
Tape #96 1 hr. $9.95

Fire Spirit with Lynn Andrews

Once again, the shamaness Andrews takes us into the wilderness of self to plumb the depths of our heart so that our being can soar. Her vision quest journey has taken her from the wilds of Manitoba to the jungles of Yucatan and the Aboriginal outback of Australia, as she attempts to bridge the gulf between the primal mind and contemporary life. As always, she expresses how we can access our natural power and move towards healing ourselves, our relationships and the planet. Her message is at once awesome and challenging.
Tape #2014 1 hr. $9.95

Crystal Dreams: Shaman Themes with Lynn Andrews

Continuing her visionary quest, the shamaness Andrews now takes us to the aboriginal wilds of the Australian outback, where she once again enters a world of limitless possibility. Here magic and mystery are the norms, and consensual reality is the aberration. Seeing the sacred, opening the heart, facing the darkness, balancing the inner male and female selves and more are all part of this extraordinary journey, as she reveals her direct experience of other realities with the Sisters of the Dreamtime.
Tape #2065 1 hr. $9.95

Finding the Sacred with Lynn Andrews

"We have very few words for aspects of the sacred," says Lynn Andrews. Here, however, she eloquently describes the essence of her own experiences with her spiritual teachers, and what it means to find sacred power within oneself. The modern shaman, she says, is anyone who survives difficult times with spiritual purpose and integrity. Aware that the authenticity of her work has been challenged, she agrees that "You shouldn't believe something you haven't experienced," and encourages us all to seek our inner being and celebrate what we already are. She is the author of many books including *The Mask of Power: Discovering Your Sacred Self* (HarperSan Francisco 1992) and *Shakkai: Woman of the Sacred Garden* (HarperCollins 1992).
Tape #2360 1 hr. $9.95

You are a vital part of the work we do!

Please become a member of "Friends of New Dimensions."

We encourage you to become a member of "Friends of New Dimensions" and help bring life-enhancing topics and ideas to the airwaves regularly. As an active member at the individual level or higher, you will receive:

- *New Dimensions* newsletter/journal, a quarterly publication containing feature articles and interviews spotlighting some of the same people and ideas you hear on our radio program, up-to-date program listings for the entire country, descriptions of new tapes, music and book reviews, and items of special interest to New Dimensions listeners.

- A 15% discount on all purchases made through New Dimensions.

Your membership contribution makes it possible to bring life-enhancing topics and ideas to the airwaves regularly, so please join at the level most consistent with your life- or work-style.

Use the order form on the following page. ⇨

New Dimensions Order Form

(U.P.S. cannot deliver to P.O. box)   Date _____

Name _____

Address _____

City _____ State _____ Zip _____

Phone _____

Tape #	Qty.	Title	Amount
1643		Medicine Woman	
1859		Walking in Balance	
1961		Earthwoman	
2014		Fire Spirit	
2065		Crystal Dreams: Shaman Themes	
2360		Finding the Sacred	
	1	Tape Catalog	FREE

Check type of payment:

☐ Check or money order ☐ Visa ☐ MC
(payable in U.S. funds)

Acct. # _____

Exp. Date _____

Subtotal	
15% membership discount	
Sales Tax Calif. res. 7.25% BART counties 7.75%	
Shipping & Handling	
Membership	
Total	

Signature—required for all credit card purchases

☐ **YES!** I want to support the radio work and become a member of "Friends of New Dimensions." I understand this entitles me to a 15% discount on all purchases from New Dimensions.

☐ Individual $35 (S721)   ☐ Radio Council: $250 (SP 72)
☐ Family: $45 (S721)   ☐ Satellite Sponsor: $500 (SP59)
☐ Sustaining: $50 (SP94)   ☐ Benefactor: $1000 (SP95)
☐ Radio Underwriter: $100 (S726)

Send order to:
New Dimensions Tapes
P.O. Box 410510
San Francisco, CA 94141-0510
Or order by telephone:
(415) 563-8899
with VISA or MasterCard
ANY TIME, DAY OR NIGHT

SHIPPING & HANDLING

If subtotal falls between	add: U.S. & Canada	Foreign
0-$15.99	$2	$6
$16-$30.99	$4	$8
$31-$50.99	$5	$10
$51-$70.99	$6	$12
$71-$100	$7	$18
over $100	$8	$25

All domestic orders are shipped 1st Class mail or UPS. All orders going outside the U.S. are shipped air. FOREIGN ORDERS: Please send an international bank money order payable in U.S. funds, drawn through a U.S. bank.

OUR GUARANTEE: All New Dimensions tapes are unconditionally guaranteed. If for any reason you are dissatisfied, you may return the tape(s) within 30 days of purchase for a full refund or exchange.

Allow one to three weeks for delivery. AB

Other Titles in the New Dimensions Books Series

Marsha Sinetar
in Conversation with Michael Toms
edited by Hal Zina Bennett

Marsha Sinetar is the best-selling author of *Do What You Love, The Money Will Follow* and *Living Happily Ever After.* In her work as an organizational psychologist, she has studied many people who have become successful doing what they love. In this new book, she speaks to those who are attempting to live their deepest calling in the midst of a seductive society. She emphasizes that choosing a lifestyle which blends inner truth with work, family and the demands of twentieth century life is more than possible—it's essential!

$8.95

Fritjof Capra
in Conversation with Michael Toms
edited by Hal Zina Bennett

In this book, Fritjof Capra takes us with him on his remarkable personal journey into the nether realms of quantum physics, where the traditional worlds of science and spirit twist and merge to the point where the distinctions become blurred. As he relates his wisdom-packed interactions with some of the leading contemporary thinkers and visionaries, from Gregory Bateson to Krishnamurti, we discover with him new ways of thinking and being.

$8.95

Patricia Sun
in Conversation with Michael Toms
edited by Hal Zina Bennett

Patricia Sun is an extraordinary teacher, human energizer and natural healer. In this book she shows how to become more aware of your intuition, and so become more trusting of the Self. With gentle directness, she encourages us to live with spontaneity, continually receptive to the creative force within us. As our words and feelings become aligned with the source of great wisdom within, we assist in the birth of a new world of harmony, cooperation and love.

$8.95

Upcoming Books in the Series:

Larry Dossey in Conversation with Michael Toms

Anne Wilson Schaef in Conversation with Michael Toms

Other Books from Aslan Publishing

Gentle Roads to Survival

by Andre Auw, Ph.D.

This is one of those rare, life-changing books that touches the reader deeply. Drawing from his forty years of counseling as a priest and a psychotherapist, Auw points out the characteristics that distinguish people who are "born survivors" from those who give up, and teaches us how to learn these vital skills. Using case histories and simple, colorful language, Auw gently guides us past our limitations to the place of safety and courage within.

$10.95

The Heart of the Healer

edited by Dawson Church and Dr. Alan Sherr

Bernie Siegel, Larry Dossey, Norman Cousins and sixteen other healing professionals here intimately describe their vision of the healing process and the innermost workings of the true healer. An inspiring and definitive review of the emerging holistic paradigm in healing.

$14.95

Intuition Workout

by Nancy Rosanoff

This is a new and revised edition of the classic text on intuition. Lively and extremely practical, it is a training manual for developing your intuition into a reliable tool that can be called upon at any time—in crisis situations, for everyday problems, and in tricky business, financial, and romantic situations. The author has been taking the mystery out of intuition in her trainings for executives, housewives, artists and others for over ten years.

$10.95

Man with No Name

by Wally Amos

In his new book *Man with No Name* Wally Amos tells of his ordeal in losing his company, his slide into financial difficulty, the tribulations of a nineteen-month lawsuit, and the principles that kept him optimistic and ultimately victorious in the midst of seemingly desperate circumstances. Amos offers an inspiring and refreshing mixture of street smarts and spiritual faith, celebrating the triumph of the human spirit over adversity.

$9.95

Other Books from Aslan Publishing

Living At the Heart of Creation

by Michael Exeter

Author Michael Exeter is one of the most important voices today for the emerging field of eco-spirituality. *Living At the Heart of Creation* pierces beyond the superficial fixes to the most pressing problems of our day. Blending profound spirituality with wide ecological knowledge, it offers remarkable insights into such challenging areas as the environmental crisis, business, relationships, and personal well-being, inspiring us to live at the heart of creation.

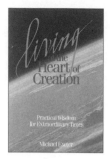

$9.95

Magnificent Addiction

by Philip R. Kavanaugh, M.D.

Kavanaugh's revolutionary work is decisively changing the way we see addictions and emotional disorders. Our unhealthy addictions aren't bad, he says—and it's a waste of time and effort to get wrapped up in getting rid of them, as he demonstrates in his own wrenching personal story. We simply need to upgrade our addictions to ones that serve us better, like addiction to wholeness, life, spontaneity, divinity.

$12.95

Personal Power Cards

by Barbara Gress

An amazing tool for retraining the negative emotions that sabotage most attempts at recovery and personal growth, *Personal Power Cards* work scientifically through colors, shapes and words to re-program the brain for maximum emotional health. Called "One of the most useful recovery tools I have seen" by *New Age Retailer*, these are a simple, incredibly quick and effective technology for building a powerful sense of self-worth in a wide variety of life areas.

$18.95

When You See a Sacred Cow... Milk It for All It's Worth!

by Swami Beyondananda

The "Yogi from Muskogee" is at it again. In this delightful, off-the-wall little book, Swami Beyondananda holds forth on the ozone layer, Porky Pig, Safe Sects, and the theology of Chocolate. Read a few lines and you'll quickly realize that nothing's safe from his pointblank scrutiny.

$9.95

Aslan Publishing Order Form

(Please print legibly)   Date _____

Name _____

Address _____

City _____ State_____ Zip _____

Phone _____

Please send a catalog to my friend:

Name _____

Address _____

City _____ State_____ Zip _____

Item	Qty.	Price	Amount
Marsha Sinetar in Conversation with Michael Toms		$8.95	
Fritjof Capra in Conversation with Michael Toms		$8.95	
Patricia Sun in Conversation with Michael Toms		$8.95	
Gentle Roads to Survival		$10.95	
The Heart of the Healer		$14.95	
Intuition Workout		$10.95	
Man with No Name		$9.95	
Living At the Heart of Creation		$9.95	
Magnificent Addiction		$12.95	
Personal Power Cards		$18.95	
When You See a Sacred Cow, Milk It…		$9.95	
	Subtotal		
	Calif. res. add 7.5% Tax		
	Shipping		
	Grand Total		

Add for shipping:
Book Rate: $2.50 for first item, $1.00 for ea. add. item.
First Class/UPS: $4.00 for first item, $1.50 ea. add. item.
Canada/Mexico: One-and-a-half times shipping rates.
Overseas: Double shipping rates.

Check type of payment:

☐ Check or money order enclosed
☐ Visa ☐ MasterCard

Acct. # _____

Exp. Date _____

Signature _____

Send order to:
Aslan Publishing
PO Box 108
Lower Lake, CA 95457
or call to order:
(800) 275-2606

NDLA